The People's Bible Teachings

CIVIL GOVERNMENT

God's Other Kingdom

Daniel M. Deutschlander

NORTHWESTERN PUBLISHING HOUSE
Milwaukee, Wisconsin

Fourth printing, 2015
Third printing, 2012
Second printing, 2001

Library of Congress Card 97-69965
Northwestern Publishing House
1250 N. 113th St., Milwaukee, WI 53226-3284
© 1998 by Northwestern Publishing House
Published 1998
Printed in the United States of America
ISBN 978-0-8100-0763-5

Table of Contents

Editor's Preface 5

Introduction 7

Part I: THE BIBLE ON CIVIL GOVERNMENT 11

    1. The Beginning of Government
       and Israel 13

    2. David, Daniel, and War 25

    3. New Testament Basics
       about Government 39

    4. Christ's Rule over Government 47

    5. Our Duty to the State 59

    6. Good Citizenship 69

    7. The Christian and Politics 75

    8. Soldiers, War, and Courts 93

Part II: THE HISTORY OF CHURCH-STATE
        RELATIONS 105

    9. From the Apostles to Constantine 107

   10. From the Middle Ages to Luther 119

   11. Luther and the Early Lutherans 129

12. Among the Non-Lutherans 143

13. From the Reformation to the Present 151

Part III: CURRENT PROBLEMS IN
         CHURCH-STATE RELATIONS 167

14. The State over against the Church 169

15. The Church over against the State 191

Endnotes 205

For Further Reading 207

Scripture Index 209

Subject Index 213

Editor's Preface

The People's Bible Teachings is a series of books on all of the main doctrinal teachings of the Bible.

Following the pattern set by The People's Bible series, these books are written especially for laypeople. Theological terms, when used, are explained in everyday language so that people can understand them. The authors show how Christian doctrine is drawn directly from clear passages of Scripture and then how those doctrines apply to people's faith and life. Most importantly, these books show how every teaching of Scripture points to Christ, our only Savior.

The authors of The People's Bible Teachings are parish pastors and professors who have had years of experience teaching the Bible. They are men of scholarship and practical insight.

We take this opportunity to express our gratitude to Professor Leroy Dobberstein of Wisconsin Lutheran Seminary, Mequon, Wisconsin, and Professor Thomas Nass of Martin Luther College, New Ulm, Minnesota, for serving as consultants for this series. Their insights and assistance have been invaluable.

We pray that the Lord will use these volumes to help his people grow in their faith, knowledge, and understanding of his saving teachings, which he has revealed to us in the Bible. To God alone be the glory.

Curtis A. Jahn
Series Editor

Introduction

The kingdom of God. Most readers of this book are familiar with that phrase. Jesus uses it repeatedly in the gospels, and the rest of the New Testament also makes frequent reference to it. Most simply defined, the kingdom of God is God's gracious rule in the hearts of believers through his Word. That kingdom is not in any one place. It is everywhere God's Word is proclaimed and his sacraments are administered according to his Word.

Closely connected to the phrase *kingdom of God* is the word *church*. In fact, the two are inseparable. The kingdom of God is God's ruling activity. The church is the sum total of all who believe the gospel.

By the preaching of the gospel, the kingdom of God is brought to people, and people are brought into the kingdom of God. Being a member of Christ's holy Christian church and being a part of the kingdom of God are one and the same thing. For by the gospel message of forgiveness won by our Savior's work, we are brought to faith; by faith Christ's kingdom is within us; and by faith we are members of his church.

Kingdom of God, church, gospel, Word and sacraments, faith in Christ: It is impossible to think of one of these without thinking of all the others. So closely are they connected that as soon as we hear the phrase *kingdom of God,* we automatically think of all the other terms as well.

But God also has another kingdom. Christ rules not only in the church but also in the world. All of history is under his feet. All kingdoms and earthly powers ultimately bow to his commands and yield to his purposes. Before his ascension Jesus himself summed up his rule: "All authority in heaven and on earth has been given to me" (Matthew 28:18). Paul sings the praises of the ascended Christ, who rules over all things for the benefit of his church: "God placed all things under his feet and appointed him to be head over everything for the church, which is his body, the fullness of him who fills everything in every way" (Ephesians 1:22,23).

Thus the rule of Christ over everything in the world, in time, and in history can be called his other kingdom. But most commonly when we talk about Christ's second kingdom, we are referring especially to civil government, to the state. That is how we will be using the term in this book.

God has placed us Christians in and under that kingdom. We have, so to speak, a dual citizenship. We are citizens of the kingdom of God through faith in the gospel promise. We are also citizens of this other kingdom by virtue of our living in this world. In the one kingdom, God rules by his Word. In the other kingdom, God rules through governments. The first kingdom gives us our permanent home in heaven and focuses our attention on spiritual matters. The second kingdom deals with our temporary but still important home on earth.

Even though the first kingdom is by far the more important one, we cannot ignore the second kingdom. God himself stands behind government and has given it power over us. God's Word tells us about the blessings he wants to give us through government. It also tells us about our responsibilities toward government.

Lutherans traditionally have taken their God-given responsibilities to the family and the church very seriously. But they have a reputation—not always undeserved—of abandoning civil government concerns to others. That frequent lack of concern is not difficult to understand. Involvement in government seems so "unspiritual," so often riddled with compromise, so subject to corruption that some Christians want nothing to do with it.

Besides that, it is often difficult to sort out the relationship between the two kingdoms. Do church and state have anything in common? Should they work together? Should they stay as far apart from each other as possible? What about prayer in public schools? What about government aid to church schools? What is the duty of someone in the kingdom of God toward the other kingdom when the state supports abortion?

Connections between church and state are close in some matters, confused in others, and at loggerheads in still others. For example, there is a "Christian Right" with one political agenda and a "Christian Left" with a very different agenda. Nor are those outside the church silent on church-and-state relationships. The noise and confusion is so great that Christians may be tempted to turn their backs on the whole discussion and wash their hands of the problem.

We, however, want to "take captive every thought to make it obedient to Christ" (2 Corinthians 10:5). Therefore let us search the Scriptures. There we will find what God has to say about his other kingdom, about civil government. There God himself will give us not a manual that answers every question but principles to guide and motivate our attitudes and actions.

With the prayer that God will bless our study of his Word, let us then ask him: What about the other kingdom? What about civil government? What about my life as a Christian citizen? What about the proper relationship between church and state?

Part I

The Bible on
Civil Government

1

The Beginning of Government and Israel

Given the importance of the two kingdoms, church and government, it may come as a surprise to discover that God does not tell us exactly how or when he established the two kingdoms. But God nevertheless stands behind both of them. He invests them with dignity and power and honor. To reject them is the same as rejecting him.

How do we account for the fact that there are no words from God that set in concrete the forms of church and state? As we observe God's ways with us, one simple truth appears again and again: God either creates a need or allows a need to arise before he meets it. We see that even in the creation account. God brought the animals to Adam *in pairs,* each with its mate. "But for Adam no suitable helper was found" (Genesis 2:20). God first made Adam aware of a need. And then, so that Adam might offer appropriate thanks, God met the need in the creation of Eve. Having satisfied the need of each for the other, God decreed how families should begin (Genesis 2:24).

The church begins

The church begins her work on the basis of a need that had already emerged in Genesis 3. There we read of man's fall into sin and of God's great grace in the first promise of the Savior. Genesis 3:15 says, "I will put enmity between you and the woman, and between your offspring and hers; he will crush your head, and you will strike his heel." The promise of the Savior created faith in Adam and Eve. The promise, however, did not put an end to sin. It is perfectly clear by the end of Genesis 4 that sin was not going to go away. It is equally clear that the promise of the Savior was not going to go away either.

The continuing presence of both sin and God's gracious promise made a need obvious. The faithful children of Adam needed and wanted to worship, to offer sacrifice. Sin needed to be addressed by God's Word of law and gospel. Heathens, even among the children of Adam, needed to hear the message of the law and the promise of the Savior. So by the end of Genesis 4, the church was functioning as believers publicly called on the name of the Lord. In public worship they confessed their faith, offered sacrifices, and proclaimed the gospel promise.

Government begins

But what about the other kingdom? What about civil government? How soon did people realize the need for civil order in their sin-corrupted society? The need for

external order became more and more obvious from Genesis 4. There we read of Abel's tragic murder by his brother.
God himself decreed the punishment for Cain and found a
way to enforce it (verses 10-16). But murder did not stop
with Cain, in spite of the punishment. Disorder increased
and so did murder. Lamech murdered someone and went
on to boast about it (verses 23,24)!

Genesis 6:11-13 tells us that by the time of Noah, the
earth was full of violence. Order had collapsed. Open corruption was so great that only the destruction of the flood
could cure it. An institution for promoting civil order was
needed—if such an institution existed, it needed drastic
reform.

After the flood, when God spoke to Noah, God
seemed to assume the emergence of government: "Whoever sheds the blood of man, by man shall his blood be
shed; for in the image of God has God made man" (Genesis 9:6). There God expressed his will that a murderer's
blood should be shed by someone. Why? Because God created us in his own image. To be sure, the essence of that
image was destroyed by the fall into sin. To be sure, the
poison of sin is passed down from generation to generation. But God had already promised the cure, the Savior,
who would crush the head of the serpent (Genesis 3:15).

By the work of the woman's offspring, our brother and
Savior, innocence and holiness would again be restored.
Through the proclamation of the promise, God had
already begun to restore his image in Adam and Eve,
Noah, and all those who called on him on the basis of the
promise. And it is God's will that those who trust in him
have his image perfectly restored in heaven.

Murder robs the victim of time to hear the promise
and share it. Murder is so monstrous that those who com-

mit it deserve to lose their own lives and the important
time for hearing and sharing the promise. Notice, however, that God does not tell us who should shed the blood
of murderers. He does not entrust the work to the victim's
family. He does not give it to the church either. He never
sanctions vigilante justice. Nevertheless, someone has to
do it. Who will that be? The task will fall to civil government, to God's other kingdom.

In the opening chapters of Exodus, the government
punishes murderers (Exodus 2:11-15). We know from both
Genesis and Exodus that early governments did more than
track down murderers for execution. In Genesis 41 to 50,
for example, God used the Egyptian government to save
his people from famine.

Unfortunately, governments often have not been the
blessing God intended. Often they have been models not
of justice but of injustice, not of peacekeeping but of violence and cruelty. That should not surprise us. The fall in
the Garden of Eden had consequences that spread through
all the institutions by which God intended to bless the
human race. It brought tragedy to the family life of Adam
and Eve. It destroyed any possibility of unity in the church,
for most people rejected the promise of the Savior and set
up their own forms of worship in direct opposition to the
Word of God. But human perversions of God's intentions
do not cancel out those intentions. God calls government
to serve as a blessing for his people and so rules history that
in spite of human perversions, God's will is done.

Civil government in Israel

The Old Testament has much more to teach us about
government than what is contained in God's words
to Noah. In the last four books of Moses, Exodus through

Deuteronomy, God himself established a government for Israel.

Israel's government was unlike any other. It had a special role to play in the history of our salvation. It was *not* a government that God gave for the whole world. It was not a government that God ever said should be imitated in all its forms and functions by other nations. It was established only for Old Testament Israel so that Israel would remain the vessel of God's gracious promise of the Savior.

God repeatedly commanded the people of Israel not to intermarry with the people of other nations because if they intermarried, they would soon fall into the idol worship of their neighbors. Such idolatry would certainly bring destruction to them, as it ultimately brings destruction to all who practice it. But something even more important was at stake. If the nation of the promise disappeared on account of intermarriage and idolatry, what would happen to the promise of the Savior? It too would disappear. How then would anyone recognize him when he came?

To keep the promise alive and to unfold it ever more clearly from generation to generation, God established a nation for the descendants of Abraham, Isaac, and Jacob. From the time of Moses until the time of Christ's appearing, God showed special grace to that nation.

Through special acts of protection and help, God showed himself as the only true God. Through prophets and plagues, he called Israel to repentance. In spite of unfaithfulness and stubbornness in Israel, he preserved the nation. Nevertheless, wickedness and unbelief in Israel became so stubborn that God finally destroyed the nation, Jerusalem, and the temple.

But after 70 years of exile, God brought the Jews back in accord with his promise. He restored their city and temple worship. God would not let the promise of the Savior perish.

Israel's constitution

What can we say about the government God created for Old Testament Israel? To answer that question, we turn to Deuteronomy, Moses' farewell address to the nation, which summarizes the whole law of God to Israel. As such it is really Old Testament Israel's constitution.

In that constitution we find basically three types of laws, with a high degree of intermingling among the three types. There was first of all *moral law*. The moral law, itself summarized in the Ten Commandments in Deuteronomy 5, is an expression of God's will for all people of all time. We see that from the repetition of the basic principles of the Ten Commandments in the words of Jesus and the apostles (Matthew 5; Galatians 5:14-26; Ephesians 5).

The second type of law given to Israel was *ceremonial law*. The ceremonial law regulated the worship life of Israel with circumcision, sacrifices, holy days, priestly rituals, and the like. Most of these ceremonies pictured the coming Savior and his work, as the epistle to the Hebrews beautifully points out. Once Jesus had come and fulfilled all the pictures of him in that law, it was abolished; it does not apply to us. Paul declares in Colossians 2:16,17: "Do not let anyone judge you by what you eat or drink, or with regard to a religious festival, a New Moon celebration or a Sabbath day. These are a shadow of the things that were to come; the reality, however, is found in Christ."

The third type of law in Israel was governmental law, or *civil law*. The civil law established a system of courts for the people (Deuteronomy 17:8-13). It provided for punishments that judges and elders would impose for crimes (16:18-20). It even had provisions for the protection of someone guilty of an accidental murder: the cities of refuge (19:1-13). It had draft laws for the army (20:1-9), economic laws about charging interest (23:19,20), and laws on marriage and divorce and inheritance (24:1-5; 25:5-10). All in all, the civil law served as a fairly comprehensive legal code.

The unique purpose of Israel's government

Again, the nation of Israel and its God-given government served a unique function in history: the preservation of the gospel promise first given in Genesis 3:15. Precisely because that function was a religious one, the government God gave to Israel mixed religious and civil functions to a very high degree. Idolatry was punishable by death (Deuteronomy 13). So was the behavior of rebellious children (21:18-21). Judges were both secular and religious (17:8-13). Unsolved murders required a religious as well as a civil resolution (21:1-9).

Because of the unique function God gave to the government of Israel, we cannot take every detail of law in Deuteronomy and apply it to governments now. Nevertheless, we can learn some things about government in general from Israel's constitution and history.

Lessons for us from Israel's government

We notice first that government and civil law assume that people are sinful and that society, therefore, will never be perfect. In fact, the assumption is that even in God's chosen nation, many, if not most, would be unbelievers. The repeated rebellions of Israel in Old Testament times amply demonstrate the accuracy of that assumption.

God wore no rose-colored glasses when he gave the civil law to Moses and Israel.

We notice second that government and civil law address *outward* behavior, not the heart. Those who hear of another's punishment may be moved to *outward* virtue; fearing punishment, some may act at least outwardly in obedience to the law (Deuteronomy 17:13).

Jesus' commentary on Old Testament civil law

Jesus commented on the purpose of Israel's civil law when the Pharisees asked him about divorce. For the sake of civil order, the law of Moses permitted divorce on relatively easy terms.

The very fact that such a law was needed to regulate outward behavior showed that many of the people were unbelievers. Jesus said, "Moses permitted you to divorce your wives because your hearts were hard" (Matthew 19:8). If hearts were pure before God and other people, there would be little need for governmental laws regulating outward behavior.

The difference between civil law and the moral law

Although God wants people to obey civil law, such obedience is not enough to make us holy before God. In Matthew 5 Jesus tells us that righteousness before God comes only through perfect obedience to a much higher standard. That standard is set by the moral law, not by civil law.

The moral law calls for perfection of the heart and then perfection in behavior. But since we lack that perfection, the moral law more than anything else shows us our sin and our desperate need for the Savior. The moral law shows us our need for help, pardon, and peace, which are found only in Christ.

Once God has shown us that no law can save us, once the gospel has shown us forgiveness in the merit of Christ alone, then God has yet another use for the moral law. It shows Christians the goal of our Christian lives as we live with one another. Our Christian lives will reflect our love to God for his grace and pardon on account of our Savior's death and resurrection for us. The first commandment of the moral law is love to God. The second flows from the first: love and service to others that reflects our love to God and our desire to serve him.

Would that all people were Christians! Would that all Christians were perfect in their love for God and knowledge of God's Word! Would that we all kept the moral law perfectly! Then there would be little need for civil law. For all the outward order that government seeks to provide would be present in a heaven of love and harmony in families and communities and even among nations. But we know that not all are Christians. We know that Christians do not always act in accord with the moral law—even though they know it. Therefore government, the other kingdom, is necessary.

Why government is necessary

Although some people may conduct their lives with outward decency, others will not. Others will cheat whenever they can. They will steal and take unfair advantage on every hand. They will strike out and even kill to get their way. For such people and such *outward* behavior, God gives power to civil government. The government with its civil law controls and curbs evil at least to some extent.

Thus God gave Israel its government and civil law to meet the needs of that nation at that time. He gave them to preserve a degree of order in the *outward* behavior of that particular mixed multitude of believers and unbelievers. He gave them as an aid to the preservation of that nation and society from which the Savior would come.

Why God gave certain penalties for crimes that we might think were not all that serious is not for us to judge. On the other hand, there is no call in the New Testament for us to campaign for the return of such penalties as those called for in Deuteronomy 19:21: "Show no pity: life for life, eye for eye, tooth for tooth, hand for hand, foot for foot."

It is enough to note that this law and its penalties were all part of a government and civil law. The purpose of this law was not salvation; its intent was not to establish righteousness before God. Its purpose and intent were to maintain outward order and control over the outward behavior of people when love to God did not motivate them.

We should note at least in passing that there is no contradiction between the moral law and the civil law in Deuteronomy. Many point to the above-cited passage, Deuteronomy 19:21, and boldly declare, "See—the Bible contradicts itself; for elsewhere the moral law tells us to forgive and love; but here the civil law tells us to get even!"

People who say such things are forgetting that the moral law and the civil law of Israel each had a different purpose and a different audience. The moral law is directed chiefly at the heart. Luther saw that very clearly and expressed it well in his Small Catechism. He begins the explanation to each of the Commandments with the words "We should fear and love God that . . ." That is the essence of the moral law: an attitude towards God that is reflected in behavior. But the civil law aims only at the outward behavior regardless of whether the person loves God.

Think of it this way: Parents tell their children to love one another and to forgive one another's slips and faults. If children always did that, there would never be any need for a parent to say, "Sam, if you don't share with Sarah, I'll have to take that toy away!" Is there any contradiction there? Not at all! The first law is addressed to the heart and behavior that flows from it; the second speaks to behavior alone after the heart has gone astray. If the first were kept perfectly, there would be no need for the second.

Thus God gives to Christians the moral law and the command to love and serve one another. But he also stands behind government and civil law, which threaten both Christians and non-Christians when behavior is loveless to the point of violence against another's life or property.

2

David, Daniel, and War

God intends that we should obey government and not rebel against it. We see in the lives of David and of Daniel and his friends especially interesting examples of believers who behaved as God wants us to behave towards civil government, its laws and officials.

David and civil government

Even though God himself had chosen Saul as Israel's first king, God rejected Saul when Saul disobeyed him (1 Samuel 15). God told Samuel to anoint David to be the new king of Israel in Saul's place (16:1-13). We might expect that David would launch a revolution as soon as possible to overthrow Saul's government. After all, wasn't

David God's appointed ruler over Israel? Hadn't Samuel promised David from the mouth of God himself that David should rule, that Saul was rejected?

But David did not start a revolution! He did not try to assassinate Saul. Even when it seemed to his friends that the moment was ripe to strike Saul, David refused (1 Samuel 24,26). Saul had become cruel, wicked, and a persecutor of the church (22:6-19). Still David refused to act against him. For God stands behind his established government, even when it fails to carry out its divinely intended purposes.

David also refused to yield to Saul's injustice. David did not just lie down and die because that's what the government wanted. *He resisted the evil of the government without falling into the evil of revolution.* That is an important and enduring principle. Revolution against even a godless government is wrong; it is a sin against God. To help the wicked in power carry out their evil intent also is wrong; it also is a sin against God.

When David could no longer serve Saul, he left. David departed not only to save his own life. His departure was also his witness to the truth that God was not behind Saul's injustice, his persecution of the church, and his cruelty. Nevertheless, David left it to God to deal with Saul. He left it to God to rule over history and to bring the day of justice for Saul's unjust government. He left it to God to keep the promise that one day David would be king.

To know where the narrow middle road lies between the God-pleasing resistance of David and sinful rebellion is not always easy. But from the behavior of David, the general principle is clear: Violence and acts of revolution against a government in power are sin—that is true even if the government is perverting God's intention for government; that is true even if the government is so perverse as to persecute the church.

We see that principle not only from David's life but also from some psalms God inspired him to write, which are prayers for God to act justly when people are unjust. In Psalm 17:13, for example, David prays, "Rise up, O LORD, confront them, bring them down; rescue me from the wicked by your sword." David had a sword of his own and the swords of many supporters. He could have sought vengeance for himself. But he was still a private citizen and not yet king. He left the matter in God's hands.

A number of psalms not only call for help from God; they also call on God to destroy and show no mercy to the enemies of the truth and the oppressors of the people (Psalms 35, 69, 109, and others).

In these psalms we see the same thought as in Psalm 17: Christians, like David, out of love to God practice obedience in their private lives; they pardon and forgive their enemies and persecutors. But Christians also pray that God in his justice will carry out justice. That *doing,* however, they leave in God's hands, for God's own time.

Thus we strive to resist evil and do good to all. By our behavior we are following this command of Christ: "Let your light shine before men, that they may see your good deeds and praise your Father in heaven" (Matthew 5:16). God has not given us any command to serve as judge, jury, and executioner of those who do not praise him. When those who live in outward wickedness and violence disturb civil order, we leave them to the government. When the government does not punish outward evil, we must leave the matter in God's hands. He will carry out justice in his own best time and way.

After Saul died and David became king, David punished evildoers and even went to war against those whom God had marked for destruction. God has given government the authority to punish the evil outward behavior of those who break the law. *As king*, David punished, not as a private citizen.

What should we do when government itself befriends evil and is the chief persecutor? We should not rebel. We should not join in the evil either. We should wait for God to avenge the blood of his people, even if we have to wait until judgment day.

God is just and carries out justice, sometimes through government, sometimes to government. But we do not carry out God's justice for him by rebellion and revolution. He never called us to that. In fact, for rebellion against Samuel's command, God rejected Saul as king in the first place (1 Samuel 15:23).

The Babylonian captivity

As we have already noted, much of what God said to the Israelites about their government does not apply to us. Their government had a unique purpose in history, which governments today do not share.

Over time the Israelites almost completely lost sight of their special function. They so despised the Word of God and the promise of the Savior that God destroyed their nation. The Northern Kingdom disappeared altogether in 722 B.C. (2 Kings 17). The Southern Kingdom was carried off into the 70-year Babylonian captivity in 586 B.C. (2 Kings 25; 2 Chronicles 36:15-23).

The believers among those taken into captivity continued to carry the promise of the Savior, but they no longer lived under a government and constitution

directly given by God. They lived under governments
that correspond much more closely to the governments
we have, at least in one respect: their laws had no direct
connection to the Bible, to the revealed will of God;
their rulers acted on the basis of natural law.

Natural law

Natural law is what is left over from the law of God
written in the hearts of Adam and Eve at creation, when
Adam and Eve knew God and his law perfectly. The fall
into sin destroyed their—and our—perfect relationship
with God. It also clouded and corrupted our ability to
know what is right and wrong, as Paul tells us in Romans
1:18-23. Conscience bears witness to the presence of natural law (Romans 2:14,15).

Those who do not have the Word of God struggle to
understand the natural law still left in the heart and to
explain why some things are right and others are wrong
and must be punished.

People try to find and understand the natural law
written in their hearts with their reasoning abilities. But
human reason is also clouded and corrupt since the fall.
With a clouded notion of what is right and wrong from
nature and with a corrupted reason trying to figure it all
out, is there any wonder that no two human law codes
agree in every point?

Most governments make laws and most rulers govern
on the basis of natural law and reason, not on the basis of
the revealed law in the Bible. What outward behavior is
good and what is bad? Reason and natural law as used by
governments declare: Good behavior best serves to keep
order and preserve society. Bad behavior undermines
order and threatens society.

Sometimes the laws of governments using natural law and reason will contain echoes of the moral law written in the Ten Commandments, just as Paul said in Romans 1:18-32. Thus rulers decree that murder is a crime because unpunished murderers are a threat to order in society. Rulers decree that stealing is a crime. With human reason people can figure out that thieves should be punished because unpunished thieves threaten social order. If thieves go unpunished, more people will steal, and fewer will work and pay taxes.

Sadly, the corruption of the natural law written in the heart and of human reason is also very evident. In Romans 1:18-32 Paul speaks of that corruption; people cover up the natural law and pervert all reason in order to do what their sinful wills want to do. That corruption is also evident in governments based on natural law and reason.

Believers under natural-law governments

The believers in the Babylonian captivity lived under governments without the revealed law of God in the Bible. They lived under rulers who had only natural law and the best interests of the state for their guides. It is useful to examine the relationship between believers and those governments.

As the Babylonian captivity was beginning, the Lord told the exiles how to behave toward the government: "Seek the peace and prosperity of the city to which I have carried you into exile. Pray to the LORD for it, because if it prospers, you too will prosper" (Jeremiah 29:7).

The believers were to submit to the government and seek the best interests of the nation. The prosperity of the nation would also be their prosperity. God's gracious intention was to bless them as they sought the peace of the city in obedience to his Word. He would bless them in their obedience, even though the Babylonian and later governments were ruled only through the use of fallen reason and clouded natural law.

Examples from the book of Daniel

The prophet Daniel and his friends give us concrete examples of how children of God behaved toward a government that held them captive. In the book of Daniel, we see repeatedly how Daniel and his friends struck a balance: They obeyed the government but also resisted injustice when the government overstepped its proper bounds.

In Daniel 3 the friends of Daniel refused to compromise the truth of God's Word. They refused to worship the statue of the king. But they did nothing that would look like the start of a rebellion. They were ready to die rather than fall into the sin of idolatry. Equally they would rather die than fall into the sin of rebellion.

Daniel himself was placed in a similar situation years later, as he tells us in Daniel 6. By that time Daniel was a very high official in the kingdom. He served the government in every way possible and sought its preservation. But look what happened when the government acted wickedly! Daniel did nothing to undermine the government, even though it had grossly overstepped its bounds. Daniel did not rebel. At the same time, he also refused to submit to the king's idolatrous decree. Like his friends Daniel was ready to suffer the consequences of faithfulness to the Word of God rather than deny it.

These Old Testament saints followed the God-given counsel of Jeremiah 29:7. They served their government faithfully. They never sought its overthrow. When God himself brought about the overthrow of Babylon and replaced it with the rule of the Medes and the Persians, Daniel served that government also.

At times both the government of Babylon and the government of the Medes and the Persians persecuted the church. At other times those governments favored the worship of the true God (Daniel 3:28,29; 4:37; 6:26,27). When they favored the worship of the true God, however, they did so for their own reasons.

To put it another way, Daniel and his friends did not campaign for the establishment of a Christian government. Nor does the sacred record tell us that they sought the persecution of unbelievers and idol worshipers. For them the concern of government ought to be *outward behavior*. Thus when the government commanded idolatry, they resisted. When they themselves were in positions of power, they did not attempt to impose their religion on others by law or force. Nor did they suppress the religion of others by law or force.

Worship is a matter of heart and conscience and therefore not a proper concern of government. *Outward behavior*, behavior that furthers the social order and security of the state, is the concern of government. Rulers and governments discover what such behavior should be from the natural law and reason.

But does that mean Daniel and his friends were indifferent to the spiritual welfare of their fellow subjects? Indeed, what could be more important for the peace and prosperity of a nation than to seek its spiritual welfare?

Daniel and his friends made a public confession of faith. It clearly moved those who witnessed it, whether to a lasting faith in the true God or not. Daniel's interpretations of the king's dreams and the writing on the wall (Daniel 2,4,5) were likewise public confessions of faith before the rulers he served.

Thus Daniel and his friends shared their faith as we do. By the pure proclamation of God's Word, they sought the best interests of their fellow citizens. But they did not use their positions of power in the government to impose their faith on anyone else by force or governmental decree. Only the Word of God can create and sustain faith.

What, then, do we notice about the lives of God's faithful children living outside Israel?

1. They did not rebel but sought the best interests of the state.

2. When the government commanded idolatry, they refused to obey but did not seek to harm the state in any way.

3. They sought the best interests of the government by faithful service to it and especially by public confession of their faith.

4. They did not expect the government to establish the religion of the true God, nor did they seek to suppress the worship of false gods with the sword of the state.

In this last point especially, we see a further refinement of the distinction we noted earlier between the moral law and civil, or governmental, law. We said that the moral law addresses the heart and expects appropriate behavior to follow. But civil law, drawn up on the basis of reason and natural law, addresses only outward behavior.

With the example of Daniel and his friends, we may observe something further about civil law: It addresses behavior toward one's fellow citizens—not behavior toward God. In the civil law of Israel, behavior toward God was also regulated: Idolatry was a civil crime, punishable by death. But Daniel and his friends demonstrate that outside Israel civil law should not deal with behavior toward God; civil law should be concerned with neither faith nor worship. When the government commanded idolatry and idolatrous worship, Daniel and his friends refused. At the same time, when they were in favor with the government, they did nothing to suppress idol worship. They confessed the one true faith, but they did not force it on anyone.

Daniel and his friends are good models of Christian citizenship. They understood well the difference between the moral law, revealed in the Ten Commandments, and civil, or governmental, law. Outside the unique circumstance of Israel, there was no expectation that government should establish worship of the one true God. Government should be concerned with behavior that threatens order in society; it should be concerned with behavior that is violent, behavior that deprives another of life or property without justice.

War in the Old Testament

A major purpose of government is the protection of its citizens. In order to carry out that purpose, government may have to wage war against those who threaten the life and territory of the nation.

The Old Testament gives us a long record of wars between nations. Sometimes wars were conducted at God's own command. Such wars were often very bloody and today would come under the heading *genocide:* God commanded the extermination of entire nations. Read Joshua, and you will see that genocide is exactly what God wanted. Indeed, read Judges, and you will see that God's judgment often fell on Israel because it was slack in carrying out his command in war. In fact, King Saul was rejected by God because he did not completely destroy the Amalekites, as God had commanded (1 Samuel 15:1-9,20-23).

The truth of these accounts in the Bible is beyond doubt or question. All Scripture is given by God's inspiration and profitable for our learning (2 Timothy 3:16). The Bible is without error, therefore, when it speaks to us about history. The commands of God with respect to war have been very troubling to many Christians, however, and at the same time have been used by unbelievers to mock Scripture: "How could a God of love and mercy command genocide? The Bible cannot be God's Word; I, at least, would not want a God who commands the extermination of entire nations!"

What shall we say in answer to troubled Christians and mocking unbelievers? We need to remember some fundamental truths about God, as he has revealed them to us in his Word. Our God is merciful beyond our understanding. He promised a Savior from the divine wrath and destruction that all deserve on account of sin. In amazing grace God gave that promise on the same day as the fall (Genesis 3:15). He revealed that the Savior would endure in his own body the punishment we deserved (Isaiah 53). He even declared that the Savior's suffering, death, and resurrection have won forgiveness and salvation for the whole world (John 1:29; 3:16; 2 Corinthians 5:18-21). Who can deny that our God is merciful and gracious beyond all reason or understanding?

But God is also just. Sin always has consequences. Adam and Eve learned that in the judgments that followed their sin (Genesis 3:16-19). Cain learned that after he murdered Abel (Genesis 4:10-12). The whole world experienced God's justice when God destroyed it with the flood, sparing only Noah and his family (Genesis 6,7). And we experience that same truth to this day; each of us could probably write a book demonstrating the observation from our own lives: Sin has consequences.

Sometimes the judgment of God as a consequence of sin is very severe. That will certainly be the case on the Last Day, when God will send to hell all those who have rejected the message of his mercy in Christ. The description of hell provided by God's unerring Word is horrible in the extreme (Matthew 25:41,46; Luke 16:19-31; Revelation 20:11-15). But those sent to hell have no one to blame but themselves. God provided the means in his Word for escape through faith in the work of his Son. He even took into account our fallen and corrupted hearts and minds; the faith he calls for in the Word is a faith he creates by the Word. Those who reject it do so out of their own stubborn rejection of the Holy Spirit's pleading in the gospel.

What, then, should we say about the judgment of God on the wickedness of people? We do not want to be found arguing with God. It is not up to us how he carries out his judgments and executes his justice on the earth. We marvel that he shows mercy and provides a way of escape in the gospel. We should not presume to tell him what he should do with those who spurn the great sacrifice of his Son.

As he will carry out his justice completely and perfectly on the Last Day, so he has carried it out in part all through history. Sometimes he acted directly, as in the case of the flood (Genesis 6,7) and the destruction of Sodom and Gomorrah (Genesis 19). More often God's acts of judgment are carried out through human agencies, especially governments. Thus it is that the government of Israel was directed by God to carry out his judgment on the wickedness of Canaan. Later God used heathen governments to carry out his judgments on unbelieving Israel (Judges 2–16; 2 Kings 17:7-23; 2 Chronicles 36:15-19).

The wars described in the Bible were terrible and bloody. The wars carried on by governments in our own day have been no less terrible and bloody. As God punished sin with sin in the destruction of Israel in the Old Testament (Jeremiah 25:8-14), so in our day he punishes wickedness and rebellion with governments that act violently, with war and oppression. His judgment in history should serve as a warning to us: God takes his Word seriously, whether we do or not, whether people like it or not!

Sadly, the innocent suffer with the guilty and cry to God for relief. So it was in Israel. So it is today. And so it will be until the end of time. God sustains the innocent and finally repays them a thousandfold what they have lost and suffered (Romans 8:18-39). That truth is hard to learn and sometimes harder still to accept. But truth it is, and truth it will remain.

Again we must marvel not at the amount of violence and cruelty inflicted on a world ripe for judgment, but at the mercy of God. For if he judged us according to our sins, we would all perish in misery. That there is destruction and judgment from God is no surprise; God is acting in justice, just as he said he would. What remains always astonishing is his patience and mercy. For by his grace alone, we have peace. From his mercy alone, we at times enjoy governments that do not pervert God's purposes for government.

The Old Testament is by no means God's last word on the subject of government, the other kingdom. Let us then move on to a consideration of the rest of what God has to say about the other kingdom, what he tells us in the New Testament.

3

New Testament Basics about Government

In the New Testament the most complete presentation on government is found in Romans 13:1-7. Even though Paul is writing to members of the church in Rome, what he says applies to all Christians, no matter where they live or what government they serve. Paul writes:

Everyone must submit himself to the governing authorities, for there is no authority except that which God has established. The authorities that exist have been established by God. Consequently, he who rebels against the authority is rebelling against what God has instituted, and those who do so will bring judgment on themselves. For rulers hold no terror for those who do right, but for those who do wrong. Do you want to be free from fear of the one in authority? Then do what is right and he will

commend you. For he is God's servant to do you good.
But if you do wrong, be afraid, for he does not bear the
sword for nothing. He is God's servant, an agent of wrath
to bring punishment on the wrongdoer. Therefore, it is
necessary to submit to the authorities, not only because
of possible punishment but also because of conscience.
This is also why you pay taxes, for the authorities are
God's servants, who give their full time to governing.
Give everyone what you owe him: If you owe taxes, pay
taxes; if revenue, then revenue; if respect, then respect; if
honor, then honor.

God established government

Because of these words from Romans 13, we call government God's other kingdom. God established government. God ultimately rules over government. Government is *God's* servant. No greater dignity could a ruler
have than that given by God in these words: "He is God's
servant" (verse 4). That is true whether the ruler knows it
or not, no matter how the ruler comes into office.

We need to emphasize this point: We owe obedience
and respect to government and government officials
because they are established by God; obedience and
respect are due because God gives them authority over us.

The proper work of government

Paul lists relatively few duties that God has given his
other kingdom, but those duties are very sweeping in their
scope. That should not surprise us. The duties of the first
kingdom, the church, are likewise described with just a
few words in the Great Commission (Matthew 28:18-20),
but who has ever fully mastered all that is contained in
that commission? Paul likewise sums up in very few words
the duties of family members (Ephesians 5:22–6:4), but in

a lifetime we will never fully master our responsibilities in the family either.

Romans 13:1-7 describes the work of the government as simply:

1. *To commend those who do good.* Notice that Paul does not define what good it is that government should commend; he leaves that to the government.

2. *To be a terror to those who do wrong.* Notice that Paul does not say the government should be a terror to those who believe wrong or to those who think wrong but to those who *do* wrong. As in the Old Testament, the business of government is *outward behavior*, not the inner workings of the soul and the heart.

3. *To carry out the punishment of those who do wrong, up to and including the death penalty.* Note the words "he does not bear the sword for nothing. He is God's servant, an agent of wrath to bring punishment on the wrongdoer" (verse 4). The sword has but two uses for the government; either it is used to execute a criminal, or it is used by a soldier in time of war. Thus wrongdoers could also be those attacking the nation in war.

4. *To collect the taxes it considers necessary to carry out its work.*

How different Romans 13:1-7 is from the law of Moses and the constitution for the nation of Israel in Deuteronomy! In the New Testament, no sweeping code of law defines for government what behavior is good and what is evil. No table of punishments is prescribed for specific crimes, nor is any attempt made to suggest ways the government might improve itself. There is not one word about what form of government would be best (for example, monarchy, dictatorship, republic, democracy) nor any specifics about economic matters, interest rates, buying and selling property, and so on. Paul's words about the duties and the dignity of government are very broad indeed.

The respect owed government

Likewise, the respect that Christians owe government is expressed in a very broad and sweeping manner. Whatever government there is has been established by God, no matter how the government has come into being. Whatever authority exists has God standing behind it.

Paul does not say only good government or governments headed by Christians are established by God. He does not say that when government does good, it should be obeyed. In fact he makes his point doubly strong: "Therefore, it is necessary to submit to the authorities, not only because of possible punishment but also because of conscience" (verse 5).

Christian consciences are formed by the Word of God. We obey and submit to God-established authority because God wants us to do so. We submit to his Word regardless of what we think or prefer or consider best with our reason.

Since God established government, rebellion is always a sin, for it is waged against the authority God himself has established. Historians might point out that rebellion almost always leaves a country worse off. But that is beside the point. Rebellion is wrong not because rebels are usually worse than the ones they seek to replace but because God tells us to submit.

Thus Christians should be obedient and peaceable citizens of the state because they know where government comes from. They know who is behind it. Yes, they know that civil government is God's kingdom, not man's.

Romans 13 is not the only place in the New Testament where God speaks to us about government. Paul later wrote similar words to Titus: "Remind the people to be subject to rulers and authorities, to be obedient, to be ready to do whatever is good" (Titus 3:1). Peter spoke in almost identical terms: "Submit yourselves for the Lord's sake to every authority instituted among men: whether to the king, as the supreme authority, or to governors, who are sent by him to punish those who do wrong and to commend those who do right" (1 Peter 2:13,14).

But . . .

A number of questions pop into our minds in the presence of these plain and simple words from the mind of God. All those questions begin with the little word *but*.

But what if the government does not do the things Paul says it should do?

Paul knew very well that government often does not do what it is supposed to do. By the time he wrote his letter to the Romans, he had already suffered persecution from the government. He suffered persecution not because of his behavior but because of his faith, because of his preaching and teaching. As we have already noted, evil *doing* is the proper concern of government; God did not give government responsibility over thinking and believing. Nevertheless, Paul leaves no room at all for rebellion, even against the unjust government under which he lived. His answer to our first question is, If government does not do what is right, that does not give Christians an excuse for doing what is wrong.

But how can a government be God's servant to us for good when it does evil, when it persecutes the church and kills Christians?

That question is as troublesome for us today as it probably was for those who first read these words of God in the epistle to the Romans. God has not given Paul or us any direct answer to the question.

As with so many truths in his Word, God tells us the *what* but not the *why*. For example, he tells us he loves us. If we ask why, his answer is, Because I chose to love you. To our way of thinking, that hardly seems to be an answer to the question. It's like asking a little boy why he ran through a mud puddle. His answer is, Oh, just because. God tells us he made us and all things. If we ask him why, his answer is, Because it pleased me to show you I love you, and I did that by creating you and giving you all that you are and have. If we ask him why he permitted evil to enter the world, his answer is, I sent my Son to redeem you from sin and death and hell.

In answer to all these questions, God tells what we need to know, not necessarily what we want to know. In telling us what we need to know, he shows us his grace and love. That is always far better than merely satisfying our curiosity!

So when we ask God how government that is evil in its deeds can be his servant, his answer essentially is this: I have told you what *you* should do. Leave to me what should be done to government that does not do what it should do!

But does that mean God wills the evil when governments do evil?

Did God move the government to kill the apostles? Did he instigate the slaughter of millions by governments through the ages? Of course not! When government does evil, it does so from the sinful nature of those in it and from the devil. Yet the government continues to be God's servant. Even when it acts wickedly, Paul states this twice for emphasis: "There is no authority except that which God has established. The authorities that exist have been established by God" (Romans 13:1).

But if government often acts wickedly and is not Christian, how can we say Christ is king? How can we say he rules over government?

This last question requires some special attention. We need to see from the Bible that (1) Christ is indeed the ultimate ruler over government but that (2) the way he rules over government differs from the way he rules over his first kingdom, the church.

In the next chapter we will consider those points first on the basis of God's promise concerning Christ the King in the Old Testament. Then we will look at what the New Testament says about Christ the King. Finally, we will examine the different ways in which Christ rules over government and the church.

4

Christ's Rule over Government

Promises concerning Christ and the other kingdom

The Old Testament promised that the Savior would be the ultimate ruler of the nations. Psalm 2 is typical of those promises. In this psalm God the Father speaks with his Son, who would become a man. As a reward for the Son's saving work, the Father promised him: "Ask of me, and I will make the nations your inheritance, the ends of the earth your possession. You will rule them with an iron scepter; you will dash them to pieces like pottery" (verses 8,9).

The book of Isaiah is filled with promises that relate to the rule of Christ over the nations. Some of the promises about Christ's rule were fulfilled by him before his birth; they were fulfilled partially when he brought back the Jews from the Babylonian captivity. But most of the promises refer especially to the rule of Christ after his earthly life, death, and resurrection. They speak of his kingship over the world, leading up to his ultimate triumph on the Last Day. Then all will see that Christ is King and Lord. Then all will know that he alone was always in control. Read Isaiah chapters 24 to 27, 45, and 60 to 66. You will see one promise after another of the Savior's triumph. You will hear one song after another in praise of him who rules over all governments, nations, and times.

All those promises in Isaiah are like the promise in Psalm 2: Jesus will rule the nations with force, with almighty power; he will rule with the violence of wars; he will rule through the destructive power of nature. By that rule over nations and governments, he will protect his church and finally deliver his people. By that rule he will both display his might to the nations and show his love to the church.

Daniel taught the same truth when he interpreted King Nebuchadnezzar's dream in Daniel 2. Daniel spoke of earthly kingdoms rising and falling in violence. But only one kingdom will remain on the Last Day, the holy Christian church. That kingdom is not made with hands nor confined to one place or time. It is a kingdom that comes from God himself and lasts forever.

All the prophets echo this same message: The promised Savior will rule over the nations. The nations may be bent on destroying the gospel and the church. At times it may even seem that they are going to succeed. But they cannot succeed. For Christ will be king over all the earth. They will perish. He will endure. His will ultimately triumphs.

The promises fulfilled

These promises are being fulfilled even now, though we do not always see their fulfillment. History is on its way to an end, and in all history Christ is King. He referred all the mentioned promises and so many others to himself when he said, "All authority in heaven and on earth has been given to me" (Matthew 28:18).

Much of Revelation is devoted to a moving picture of Christ and his rule over the world. Always that rule is pictured heading toward one goal: the triumph of Christ and his saints on the Last Day. But on the way to that goal, the opponents of the gospel often appear to be winning.

Paul loved to write of Christ's rule over the nations and kingdoms of the world and did so even when he was suffering persecution from the government. How glorious is the picture of Christ that Paul paints for us in Philippians 2:6-11!

> [Christ Jesus], being in very nature God, did not consider equality with God something to be grasped, but made himself nothing, taking the very nature of a servant, being made in human likeness. And being found in appearance as a man, he humbled himself and became obedient to death—even death on a cross! Therefore God exalted him to the highest place and gave him the name that is above every name, that at the name of Jesus every knee should bow, in heaven and on earth and under the earth, and every tongue confess that Jesus Christ is Lord, to the glory of God the Father.

After the triumph of our Savior in death and resurrection, he now lives exalted over all things for all times; all must ultimately bend the knee before him, whether in faith or in fear, and confess that he is Lord alone!

In Ephesians 1:18-22 Paul rejoices in the rule of Christ the King:

> I pray also that the eyes of your heart may be enlightened in order that you may know the hope to which he has called you, the riches of his glorious inheritance in the saints, and his incomparably great power for us who believe. That power is like the working of his mighty strength, which he exerted in Christ when he raised him from the dead and seated him at his right hand in the heavenly realms, far above all rule and authority, power and dominion, and every title that can be given, not only in the present age but also in the one to come. And God placed all things under his feet and appointed him to be head over everything for the church.

Paul's rejoicing was not caused by what he was experiencing. Imprisonment and ultimately death were his lot from worldly rulers. In fact that's what Jesus had promised Paul from the start (Acts 9:16). No, Paul rejoices because in every circumstance Christ still rules and carries out his rule for the benefit of the church, yes, the benefit even of his suffering and dying apostle!

In Colossians 1:15-18 Paul again sings the praises of Christ as the one who rules without limit over all that exists and as the one for whom all things exist.

> He is the image of the invisible God, the firstborn over all creation. For by him all things were created: things in heaven and on earth, visible and invisible, whether thrones or powers or rulers or authorities; all things were created by him and for him. He is before all things, and in him all things hold together. And he is the head of the body, the church; he is the beginning and the firstborn from among the dead, so that in everything he might have the supremacy.

Beautiful indeed are the passages of promise in the Old Testament and the hymns of praise in the New Testament that speak of Christ the King!

Notice the emphasis in all these passages that speak of Christ's rule over nations and governments. The way he rules over nations is very different from the way he rules over the church. His rule over the other kingdom may be summed up this way:

1. He rules over the nations without personally revealing himself. Most of the time nations and governments are ignorant of him and his Word; that he is the real ruler is hidden from their eyes.

2. He rules over the nations without their consent. Often they even violently oppose him and his Word, which will triumph in the end, however.

3. He does not explain to the nations *or to us* exactly how his almighty rule is being carried out when nations and governments oppose him, act wickedly, and persecute the church. He only tells us that he is in control and ultimately will triumph and that his control is *always* for the benefit of believers, whether they can see it or not (Romans 8:31-39)!

4. He calls on believers to trust his Word that he is King over all the earth whether they see his rule or not. Because he is King, they are to obey those to whom he has given the sword of government; to refuse obedience is to rebel against him, the true and only real King.

Nations and governments serve his purposes

Governments and nations serve Christ's purpose even when they are not aware of it, even when they oppose his church. When his purpose has been served, he ultimately judges and destroys them. His judgment most often takes the form of natural calamity and war. He does all in his own time, when it pleases him. He then raises up other governments to take their place.

For example, he sent the Babylonians to punish the wickedness of Israel. Then he sent the Medes and Persians to punish the wickedness of the Babylonians. Babylonian and Persian rulers thought they were doing just as they pleased. Most of the time the rulers did not know their coming and going was all part of God's plan to save his people. They did not know they were servants of Christ the King.

In the years before the New Testament, God raised up the Greeks. They gave the Mediterranean world a common language; later that would serve in the spreading of the gospel. Then God raised the Romans; through them he provided a unified government for the Mediterranean world, which also aided in the spreading of the gospel. But it never occurred to the Greeks and Romans at the time that their chief purpose in history was the advance of the gospel. That was all the doing of Christ the King.

Government for its own reasons crucified our Savior, its King. In so doing, the Roman governor knew he was acting unjustly. The Jewish government acted wickedly and illegally as well. But Christ the King accomplished his saving purposes in spite of the wicked intentions of the Roman and Jewish officials.

In all these instances, governments unknowingly submitted to Christ the King. They submitted to his will, even though they often intended the opposite.

This rule of Christ over governments is altogether different from his rule over the church. In order to see the

contrast as clearly as possible, let us sum up also how he
rules over the church:

1. Christ reveals himself to the church with his Word
   of the gospel. He invites and calls us to himself with
   the message of forgiveness: "Come to me, all you who
   are weary and burdened, and I will give you rest"
   (Matthew 11:28).

2. Christ rules over the church, over believers, by giving. He gives eternal life through the message of the
   gospel: "I am the resurrection and the life. He who
   believes in me will live, even though he dies; and
   whoever lives and believes in me will never die"
   (John 11:25,26). By those gifts he sets up his royal
   throne in our hearts.

3. The church knows Christ by his Word and wants to
   be ruled by him through his Word. By faith the
   church knowingly and willingly follows him: "Lord,
   to whom shall we go? You have the words of eternal
   life. We believe and know that you are the Holy One
   of God" (John 6:68,69).

4. Through Word and sacraments, Christ creates an
   intimate bond of love, a union, a communion
   between himself and his church. "We were therefore
   buried with him through baptism into death in order
   that, just as Christ was raised from the dead through
   the glory of the Father, we too may live a new life"
   (Romans 6:4). "Is not the cup of thanksgiving for
   which we give thanks a participation in the blood of
   Christ? And is not the bread that we break a participation in the body of Christ?" (1 Corinthians 10:16).

The two kingdoms are distinct

Could the contrast between church and state be any
more striking? The two are distinct kingdoms, even

though Christ is King over both. The two kingdoms are separate, even though Christ rules over governments and nations always and only for the benefit of his believers. It is not our job to separate the two kingdoms. They already are separate by virtue of the very different ways in which Christ rules over them.

We have seen that the ways in which he establishes and rules in church and state are very different. So also the work he has given each to do is different. And the tools they use for their work are different as well.

As we have seen from Romans 13, the work of the government is the punishment of evildoers and the commendation of those who do good. That work is very important, but it is also a work that lasts only for this life. The tool God has entrusted to the government is "the sword" (Romans 13:4); government accomplishes its work with the threat of punishment for those who resist.

The work of the church, on the other hand, is the proclamation of the gospel (Matthew 28:18-20). That work has eternal benefits. It brings forgiveness and spiritual strength for this life and, finally, life eternal in heaven. The only tool God gives for this work is the saving message of the gospel. The message itself creates and sustains saving faith, because Christ can never be separated from his Word. He gives himself to us in it and brings us to himself through it (Isaiah 55:10,11; John 6:35-40; Romans 10:14-20; 1 Corinthians 12:3).

Could the two kingdoms be more different? One has territory on a map; the other exists in hearts. One is concerned only with bodily and temporal matters; the other is chiefly concerned with spiritual and eternal matters. One is concerned only with outward behavior; the other always is concerned first with the attitude that motivates the behavior. We enter one by a visible, physical birth; we enter the other invisibly, through a spiritual rebirth, through the door of faith in the gospel promise, which the Holy Spirit created in us through Baptism. In one kingdom we die; in the other we live forever.

Jesus demonstrated the separation of the two kingdoms

The strong contrast between Christ's rule in the first kingdom and his rule in the second can be seen in all of Christ's life on earth. The separation he wants believers, his church, to respect is evident in the whole work of our salvation. Consider Philippians 2:5-8:

> Your attitude should be the same as that of Christ Jesus: Who, being in very nature God, did not consider equality with God something to be grasped, but made himself nothing, taking the very nature of a servant, being made in human likeness. And being found in appearance as a man, he humbled himself and became obedient to death—even death on a cross!

When Christ became man, what did he do? He humbled himself and became a servant of servants. He entered what we call his *state of humiliation.* He hid the glory that was his from before the world began. He veiled his almighty power under the mask of a lowly human nature. By his humiliation even to death, death on a cross, he redeemed the world. By that death for us and by the lowly gospel message, he established and preserves the church.

Notice, however, that Paul begins the description of Christ's humiliation with the call "your attitude should be the same as that of Christ Jesus" (verse 5). Those words are addressed to believers; they are addressed to the church. They are not addressed to earthly kingdoms and governments, whose job it is to rule.

Just as Christ the King, Lord of the nations, showed himself on earth in lowliness and humility, so the church, his bride, should imitate him in lowliness and humility. The church on earth, not the government, follows Christ in his humiliation; she waits for him to exalt her after this life.

Jesus himself is the pattern. First he suffered and died; then his human nature was exalted after his death and in his resurrection (Philippians 2:9-11). For the church to expect to rule in this life is to set aside humiliation for glory. That's not the will of Christ; it's not the pattern he set for the church on earth. Worldly power is for worldly governments; lowliness, humility, and suffering in imitation of the Savior is for the church as she follows in his footsteps.

Again, Jesus' earthly life demonstrated the separation between the two kingdoms time after time. His whole attention during his earthly life was devoted to redeeming us and thus to the creation of the church through the gospel. Consider how often Jesus refused to use his kingship over governments and the world in order to accomplish our salvation and create the church:

1. Shortly after Jesus' birth, he became a refugee. His family fled from the wicked king Herod (Matthew 2:13-15). Jesus did not use his power to strike down Herod and his soldiers. In order to fulfill the Scriptures, he suffered in lowliness at the hands of the government even as an infant!

2. At the very beginning of Jesus' public ministry, he refused the devil's temptation to use worldly power and might (Matthew 4:8-10). The devil came to offer him an easy way to win the world: no cross, no crown of thorns, no suffering and death. The devil promised that Jesus could have all the kingdoms of

the world for just one act of idolatry. Instead, the Savior chose the way of the cross!

3. After Jesus fed the five thousand, the crowd wanted to make him an earthly king (John 6:14,15). He showed his refusal by quickly sending his disciples to the boat (Matthew 14:22); he did not want them to be carried away with enthusiasm for the idea. Then he went alone to a mountain to pray (John 6:15).

4. When Peter urged Jesus not to go the way of the cross, Jesus rebuked him (Matthew 16:21-23). Willingly the Savior embraced suffering and death instead of outward power and glory.

5. Jesus allowed himself to be arrested, tried by two courts, mocked and scourged by soldiers, and crucified at the command of the government.

Especially in the events surrounding his suffering and death, Jesus declared himself king over all things, even over death. In the Garden of Gethsemane, Jesus reminded Peter that the angels were still at his beck and call (Matthew 26:52-54). Even before that, Jesus declared that his life could not be taken from him; he would give it up freely (John 10:17,18). He did not die because he had lost his power and his kingship. Instead, he used his control over history to guarantee that no one would prevent his march to the cross for our salvation.

Perhaps most instructive of all are the words Jesus spoke during his trials before the Sanhedrin and Pilate. Jesus declared, "I say to all of you: In the future you will see the Son of Man sitting at the right hand of the Mighty One and coming on the clouds of heaven" (Matthew 26:64). With these words Jesus declared for all to hear that he was indeed King of kings and Lord of lords, the real ruler of heaven and earth.

Only hours later Jesus made the point crystal clear before Pilate: He had not come to establish an earthly kingdom of power and might. Jesus told Pilate: "My kingdom is not of this world. If it were, my servants would fight to prevent my arrest by the Jews" (John 18:36).

In summary: Christ is King; he rules over two distinct kingdoms in very different ways. He gives each its proper work and the tools for carrying out that work. He has placed us by the gospel in the kingdom of the church; he has placed us by physical birth in the other kingdom. He accomplishes his will in both kingdoms.

In the kingdoms of this world we often have difficulty seeing how that is so. Nevertheless, it is so. Jesus' own life is the best proof: Jewish and Roman governments thought they were getting their way when they crucified him; but by his lowliness, his suffering and death, he earned our salvation. And in his resurrection he proved his rule over all, even over death.

We are often like the disciples when we try to figure out how Christ is ruling over nations. The disciples had difficulty seeing the sense in Christ's suffering when it was happening. But after Jesus rose from the dead and sent the Holy Spirit at Pentecost, he made it all clear to them. Likewise he will finally make his rule over this other kingdom clear to us. He does that in part now when we study history and see how he has kept his Word. But he does it only in part. The many things in history that still baffle us he will make clear in heaven. That was Paul's confession and confidence: "Now we see but a poor reflection as in a mirror; then we shall see face to face. Now I know in part; then I shall know fully, even as I am fully known" (1 Corinthians 13:12). May it be our confession and confidence too!

5

Our Duty to the State

We have seen that Christ is indeed King in both the church and the state. Let us then resume our consideration of our duty to the other kingdom, the state. As we have already noted in Chapter 3, our first duty to the state is obedience. But our duty does not end there. Paul tells us that we owe respect as well as obedience.

Respect

The respect we give to officials of government has to do with their office, not their person. Nero, one of the emperors in Paul's day, was a scoundrel of the worst sort. He burned Rome for the sake of his own urban renewal project and then blamed the Christians for the fire. He even tried to kill his own mother. Paul did not need to respect the emperor as a person. But he did need to respect him on account of his office.

We may have some officials in our day whom we respect personally. But we may also know of officials whose lives are worthy of no respect at all. Nevertheless, whether rulers are of noble character or scoundrels, God stands behind their office and their work. Their authority comes from Christ the King. They may not recognize his kingship, but we do. To respect them is to show reverence to Christ the King, who gave them their authority.

Christ himself set the perfect example. Not one word of disrespect came from his mouth when he stood before the courts of the Jews, Herod, and the Romans. The apostle Peter reminds us of it: "When they hurled their insults at him, he did not retaliate; when he suffered, he made no threats. Instead, he entrusted himself to him who judges justly" (1 Peter 2:23).

Paul also serves as a good example. He knew that his judges might be unjust. But in all his court appearances, he showed respect for the authority placed over him, even when the persons merited only God's judgment (Acts 23:1-5).

Outside the Bible Martin Luther is perhaps the best example of one who showed respect for governmental rulers. He had few illusions about the persons of princes and of the emperor. He remarked once that a prince would be a rare treasure in heaven. He had seen often how many of them behaved unjustly, with cruelty, and completely contrary to the Word of God. Nevertheless, what does he say of our attitude toward rulers and officials of the state? In his Large Catechism, he writes:

In the same way we speak about the parental estate and civil authority. If we regard these persons with reference to their noses, eyes, skin and hair, flesh and bones, they look no different from Turks and heathen. Someone might come and say, "Why should I think more of this person than of others?" But because the commandment is added, "You shall honor father and mother," I see another man, adorned and clothed with the majesty and glory of God. The commandment, I say, is the golden chain about his neck, yes, the crown on his head, which shows me how and why I should honor this particular flesh and blood.[1]

Taxes

We also owe taxes to the state. Paul mentioned taxes in Romans 13. If anyone had an excuse to dodge the payment of taxes, it was Paul. Taxes were collected by "tax farmers" who bought the right to collect taxes for the government. They had a set amount that was sent to the government, but they could collect as much as they could get away with collecting. The army stood behind them. Thus the tax actually paid was only a percentage of what was collected. Still worse, the tax was used to pay the very officials and soldiers who arrested and executed Christians.

Not one word from Paul justifies any kind of tax evasion, however. Again, submission to the government is the principle. We may see the government use taxes in ways that offend and outrage us. We may see the government use taxes in ways that are completely contrary to the Word of God. For example, taxes pay for godless teaching as well as good teaching in public schools. Taxes also may fund abortion, which is murder in our eyes as well as in God's eyes. Taxes may support a system of justice that is often unjust. But if Paul had no advice to give the Christians in his day about avoiding taxes, how could we possibly find an excuse in our day? Once again, submission belongs to us; judgment belongs to God.

The government does not do only evil. Government uses the sword in punishing evildoers and in protecting the state, as Paul pointed out in Romans 13. When the early Christians paid their taxes, they could console themselves that they were supporting what God has given government to do. That is our consolation too, which may help. But ultimately the reason why we pay taxes is because our King and Savior has told us to do so. We noted Paul's words earlier: "It is necessary to submit to the authorities . . . because of conscience" (Romans 13:5). That conscience is not formed by our feelings nor by our reason. It is formed by the Word of our God.

These are hard lessons to learn: obedience, respect, payment of taxes. But we want to remember that this is the will of Christ. He gave obedience and respect. He even paid taxes (Matthew 17:24-27). We render obedience and respect to Christ when we respect and obey those he has placed over us. Ultimately it is even to Christ that we render taxes, for he is King.

That perhaps is one of the points worthy of note in Matthew 22:15-21. In answering a trick question of the Pharisees about taxes, Jesus concluded by saying, "Give to Caesar what is Caesar's, and to God what is God's" (verse 21). What is it that belongs to God? Everything! *Everything* includes Caesar, that is, the government. When we give to Caesar what is Caesar's, we also give to God what is God's.

Prayer

In 1 Timothy 2:1,2 Paul gives us yet another duty we owe the government. He writes, "I urge, then, first of all, that requests, prayers, intercession and thanksgiving be

made for everyone—for kings and all those in authority,
that we may live peaceful and quiet lives in all godliness
and holiness."

God wants us to pray for the state and for rulers. He
promises to hear us when we pray. Do we live in a land
where we are able to "live peaceful and quiet lives in all
godliness and holiness"? Then God has answered our
prayers. To him we give all thanks and praise that he has
prospered the state so we would have that blessing!

Paul adds this significant thought: "This is good, and
pleases God our Savior, who wants all men to be saved
and to come to a knowledge of the truth" (1 Timothy
2:3,4). What great incentives these are both to pray for
the state and to live godly and holy lives in it! It pleases
God! What more could we want?

But even beyond that, Paul implies that such answered
prayers are also most useful for the missionary work of the
church. God saves us by his Word as it is proclaimed, and
his earnest will is that people hear the gospel and by its
power believe it. Mission work is easier to do when the
state prospers and is at peace than when the state is in turmoil and chaos.

Finally, when we live quiet and peaceable lives in our
country, we witness to the peace within that comes from
the gospel. For many whose hearts are full of darkness and
confusion, the peaceful and godly life of a Christian may
become a magnet to the gospel source.

Limitations on the power of the other kingdom

We have seen that the powers of the government are
stated in very general terms in the Bible. But examples
from the New Testament and the Old Testament also
show that there are limits on governmental power.

We noted earlier that the civil law governed outward behavior in the Old Testament. We have also seen from Romans 13 and from 1 Peter 2 that the proper concern of government in New Testament times is also outward behavior. God has not given the government rule over hearts and thoughts. Faith is not the proper business of the government, any more than the sword is the proper business of the church.

Christians must always respect government. For conscience' sake they dare never rebel. But there are times when Christians must resist government. We see that in the example of the Hebrew midwives in Exodus 1. They refused to kill the male babies, as Pharaoh had ordered. God blessed them because they feared him more than the king. We see the same thing in the examples of David and Daniel. When King Saul tried to kill David, David did not rebel, but he did resist. When King Nebuchadnezzar tried to force Daniel's friends to worship a false god, they did not rebel, but they did resist. When King Darius issued a decree forbidding prayer, Daniel did not rebel, but he did resist. We see the same as well in the examples of the apostles in Acts 5 and Paul's ministry. Perhaps the simplest way to summarize it is this:

1. When the government tries to be the church, the Christian must resist.

2. When the government tries to force a Christian into behavior contrary to the Word of God, the Christian must resist.

When the government tries to be the church . . .

Government tries to be the church when it intrudes into matters of the soul. If government makes laws concerning faith and worship, it is intruding into work that God has not given to government but to the church.

Even if the state wanted to order everyone to believe the Word of God, the state would be wrong to do so. Remember Daniel: He refused to worship the government's false god, but when he had the power, Daniel also refused to force anyone to worship the true God. God has not given matters of faith to the state. He has given the sword to the state, not the gospel and not the sacraments. Also in the New Testament, we have many examples of government trying to force matters of faith and worship. In Acts 5 the Jewish high court ordered the apostles to stop preaching and teaching the gospel. The apostles' answer was simple and crystal clear: "We must obey God rather than men!" (verse 29). Even though the apostles were flogged and the order was repeated, they refused to obey. "Day after day, in the temple courts and from house to house, they never stopped teaching and proclaiming the good news that Jesus is the Christ" (verse 42).

Paul's entire ministry, as recorded in Acts, makes the same point. Again and again the enemies of the gospel enlisted the power of the state; they wanted the state to prevent Paul from preaching and teaching the Word of God. But Paul resisted. He remained faithful to the Word and to his apostolic call.

The examples of the apostles in Acts 5 and of Paul's ministry demonstrate a boundary the government should not cross. If governments command disobedience to the revealed will of God in the Bible, Christians will obey God rather than men. God has called us to worship him alone. He has called us to make proper and holy use of his name. He has called us to gladly hear and share his Word. The state is not free to forbid what God commands.

Could it happen in our day that government might try to interfere in the work of the church? Could government in our day go beyond the judging of criminal behavior to the business of judging souls or the Word of God? That is not at all out of the realm of possibility. Perhaps teachers face this threat more obviously than anyone else. What must a Christian public school teacher do if the government insists that the creation account in Genesis be rejected and ridiculed? if the school board requires a family life or family planning curriculum that is contrary to the Fourth and Sixth Commandments? if counsel is sought by a pregnant student? Must the teacher suggest the possibility of abortion, even though the mother's life is not threatened?

We will consider many more problems of this sort later. For now, the examples mentioned may be sufficient to raise awareness to the problem: We still live in a world where conflicts between the Christian and the government arise. These problems do not exist only in other countries. They exist in North America too.

The Word of God calls us to make a bold confession of our faith. It calls us not to compromise its truth. Jesus himself gives a stern warning to those who refuse that call: "Whoever acknowledges me before men, I will also acknowledge him before my Father in heaven. But whoever disowns me before men, I will disown him before my Father in heaven" (Matthew 10:32,33).

We do not expect and we do not want the government or its schools to preach the gospel and try to save souls. That is not the government's business. But we do not want the government to force teachers and students to ridicule the Bible and its teachings either. When the government attempts to teach religion, whether it is true religion or—

as is much more likely—false religion, the Christian must obey God rather than men.

Again, it is important to note that the apostles did *not* call for a rebellion against the governments that persecuted them. But it is equally important to note that when the government tried to act like a church, the apostles refused to obey; they resisted. For the government cannot command disobedience to the Word of God any more than it can command faith in the Word of God. Especially the first three commandments deal with our relationship to God on the basis of God's Word alone. Those commandments are not the business of the government. They are the concern of the church and of the individual believer.

When the government tries to force a Christian to sin . . .

Peter and the other apostles applied the principle "We must obey God rather than men!" when the government tried to forbid the preaching and teaching of God's Word in its truth and purity. The principle would also apply to governmental actions contrary to commandments other than the First, Second, and Third. If the government tried to force a Christian doctor to perform an abortion contrary to the Word of God, the Christian doctor would have to refuse. The doctor might well look to the example of the Hebrew midwives in Exodus 1. If the government ordered a Christian soldier to murder innocent captives or civilians, the soldier would have to refuse.

A confession to the truth may be very costly for the one making it, as it was for the apostles and the early Christians. But our Lord has promised us that exactly such conflicts will arise for the Christian. Read all of Matthew 10. You will see that Christ never promised the believer an easy time. Again, the church imitates Christ in his state of humiliation here on earth. The time of exaltation is for us as it was for Christ—after suffering and death. It is for the resurrection. It is for heaven.

Christ is King in the church and in the hearts of her members by the gospel. Christ is King over the nations and over governments to whom he has entrusted the sword. His rule over both is assured by his resurrection and ascension. His triumph, however, remains hidden until he makes all things clear in heaven.

To the church and state, Christ the King has given different work and different tools for accomplishing that work. As members of an eternal kingdom and citizens of an earthly kingdom, we have responsibilities to both. In the following chapters, we will examine more closely our lives as Christians in the earthly kingdom.

6

Good Citizenship

In this chapter and the next two, we will consider how the individual Christian should conduct himself or herself in the earthly kingdom. God's will is not that we separate ourselves from it. Our Lord Jesus prayed the following for us in his great high priestly prayer:

> My prayer is not that you take them out of the world but that you protect them from the evil one. They are not of the world, even as I am not of it. Sanctify them by the truth; your word is truth. As you sent me into the world, I have sent them into the world. (John 17:15-18)

In the world but not of it

We are not in heaven yet. Nor does Jesus command us to set up some sort of separate society on earth, far removed from unbelievers and all that might harm us.

We are in the world, Jesus says, but we are not of the world. That is, we do not live like the animals, which have no other home than this world. Nor do we live as though we have evolved from some microbe in the dust. No, we live as permanent citizens of heaven. We live as those who have been begotten by the water of Baptism and the Word of the gospel. We live as those with an eternal destiny and goal: life in heaven with Jesus, the angels, and all the saints. This world is not our home. We are foreigners here with a temporary visa.

Our stay here is long enough and important enough, however, for us to be reckoned citizens. As temporary citizens of this world, we want to know how our Savior and King would have us live in it.

The Great Commission (Matthew 28:18-20) always holds before us our chief assignment: to hold firmly to God's Word, teach it in all its truth and purity, and share it with all in the world.

In the Sermon on the Mount, Jesus tells us that a big part of such holding to his Word is the life we lead in the society in which we live. He says: "You are the light of the world. . . . Let your light shine before men, that they may see your good deeds and praise your Father in heaven" (Matthew 5:14,16).

A pattern for the Christian citizen

Our lives in the earthly kingdom, therefore, are to reflect our loyalty to the Word of God. Our lives are to bring him honor. Peter exhorts us:

> It is God's will that by doing good you should silence the ignorant talk of foolish men. Live as free men, but do not use your freedom as a cover-up for evil; live as servants of God. Show proper respect to everyone: Love the brother-

hood of believers, fear God, honor the king. Slaves, submit yourselves to your masters with all respect, not only to
those who are good and considerate, but also to those who
are harsh. For it is commendable if a man bears up under
the pain of unjust suffering because he is conscious of
God. But how is it to your credit if you receive a beating
for doing wrong and endure it? But if you suffer for doing
good and you endure it, this is commendable before God.
To this you were called, because Christ suffered for you,
leaving you an example, that you should follow in his
steps. (1 Peter 2:15-21)

Everywhere in the Bible we see this same pattern. We
are to live peaceably with our neighbors, whether they are
Christians or not. We are to work honestly and faithfully
for those who employ us, whether they are honest and
faithful or not. We are to be obedient and respectful
toward the government, whether it always acts as it ought
or not.

That means we obey the law of the land. We sign contracts and keep our word. We tell the truth on tax forms
and in court. The excuse of the heathen that dishonesty is
only wrong if one gets caught should not be part of a
Christian's way of thinking. Even simple things like obedience to traffic laws are part of Christian citizenship. Disobedience to the law of the land is disobedience to God.

To be sure, the laws of the land can sometimes be so
complicated that complete obedience is impossible. In
some countries that complexity is deliberate. The former
Soviet Union, for example, had laws that were not published or made public; that way a citizen could always be
hauled in by the police, even if no apparent law had been
broken. Currency laws in many countries likewise fit into
the category of laws almost impossible to keep.

Even in countries that are not totalitarian, the rules and regulations of governmental agencies, tax laws, and contract laws can be mind-boggling in their complexity. Nevertheless, Christians need to recognize that during their pilgrimage in the earthly kingdom, they are subject to the laws of that kingdom.

Out of loyalty to their true King, Christians want to make every effort to obey, even when the laws may appear senseless. Out of love to Christ, we willingly endure the difficult challenges to our faith; shall we not from the same love put up with the petty and the merely inconvenient?

The ultimate reasons for good citizenship

This entire attitude and behavior toward the world should be the result of Christ's saving work for us. Because he has loved us and given himself for us, we want to do what he wants us to do. He wants us to live in an honorable way in the world for two reasons: (1) it pleases him, since it is according to the holy law of God; (2) it serves the ultimate purpose of aiding in the spread of the gospel message.

Paul makes the same points in words we considered earlier, 1 Timothy 2:2. He reminds us to pray for all those in authority, "that we may live peaceful and quiet lives in all godliness and holiness." You may recall that Paul closely connects these words with a missionary purpose: "This is good, and pleases God our Savior, who wants all men to be saved and to come to a knowledge of the truth" (1 Timothy 2:3,4).

When we lead godly lives, we become in part God's answer to our prayers for the government and those in authority. So far as we are good and honorable citizens, the government is strengthened, society is more peaceful, and our ability to share the gospel under peaceful circum-stances is enhanced.

In summary: Our lives in society and under govern-ment serve our neighbor. To live other than God's Word has directed harms our neighbor. If we were to be disor-derly, society would be the more disorderly, to our neigh-bor's harm. If we were to separate ourselves from society, we would do our neighbor no good. If we were to live as greedy, malicious, self-seeking worldlings, we would drive our neighbor away from the gospel we profess to love. If we were to take no part in government, we would risk leaving it to those who serve only themselves, which also would hurt our neighbor.

We have already discussed some of the more general ways in which Christians serve government. We obey and respect it within the limits set by the Word of God. We pay taxes. We pray for the government. We never rebel against it, even though at times we may have to resist it. But there are other ways in which we can serve the gov-ernment and thus serve also our neighbor. The ways listed so far have been personal or private ways for the most part. Other ways are more public. They are also more compli-cated. We will look at some of them in the next chapter.

7

The Christian and Politics

The governments under which we live are very different from the governments of biblical times. The apostles and prophets lived in countries where the laborer or farmer had virtually no influence on the government, but we live in countries with democratic institutions. We have a right to vote. We have a right to petition the government. We have a right to campaign for public policies and political candidates.

While carrying out our responsibilities as citizens of the nation, we will want to be careful that we do not mix church and state in the process. The goal of our political activities must never be the creation of the kingdom of God on earth, because God creates his kingdom on earth through the gospel, not the government.

At the same time, when we vote, campaign for a candidate, or hold office, we act as Christians. We never want to leave the Word of God behind in anything we do. So we don't want to leave it behind when we serve the state either.

How do we keep our political lives or activities from becoming attempts to mix church and state?

A basic principle on which government rests

In Chapter 1 we discussed natural law. Governments are set up largely on the basis of natural law—what is left of the moral law, which God wrote in the hearts of Adam and Eve at creation. People without the Bible use their reason to figure out what the natural law is, what is right and wrong. Reason and natural law are closely tied together. Conscience sits as judge over our actions in large part on the basis of natural law.

We want to consider now the importance of reason in governmental decisions. We need to understand reason's role and what use Christians can make of reason and natural law when they enter the political arena. Doing so will help us act as Christian citizens who do not want to mix up church and state.

Governments run on the gasoline of natural law and human reason, not on the living water of the Word of God. This basic principle applies to all types of government: republics, monarchies, parliamentary democracies, and dictatorships. God has given none of them his Word. As we have noted repeatedly, he has given the Word and sacraments to the church, not the state. So when governmental leaders make decisions, where do they go for guidance? They make decisions on the basis of human reason.

Likewise, most voters cast their ballots on the basis of reason; each voter thinks his or her choice is rational.

The example of the school board

Let's consider an example of that principle in action. How will members of a public school board decide issues of curriculum for the schools in their district?

Some parts of a potential curriculum might be controversial. What about the creation account in Genesis? Will that be mentioned, taught as a possibility, ignored, or ridiculed?

What about family life? Will birth and death be taught from the view of those who deny the existence of God? Will an unborn child be thought of as nothing more than tissue, the result of glands and hormones? Will death be presented as the end of existence? Will homosexuality be presented as an alternative lifestyle?

What about history? Will the goal of the textbook be to teach good citizenship, nationalism, and patriotism? Will it hide the national warts and blemishes? Or will it do the opposite and make the dominant culture the villain and cause of all that is wrong in the world? Will it ignore the role of the church? Or will it mention Christianity as one of the great world religions, as good as any other, perhaps no worse?

After the school board has listened to those considered experts, how will it decide these difficult questions? The most important consideration will probably be the will of the majority of voters. Of course, that majority view will have to be weighed against the rights of the minority. It will also have to be weighed against current laws. Court rulings on school matters will have to be taken into account. Personal opinions of the members also will play some role.

All these are rational considerations. When members cast their votes, each one will think he or she is voting for the most reasonable course of action.

The example of legalized gambling

Consider another example. The legislature is trying to decide whether to legalize gambling. How will the legislators make up their minds on which way to vote?

Some will consider the majority opinion in their district. Some will ask themselves about the relative benefits to state coffers from gambling revenue. Some will decide on the basis of damage done to those who become addicted to gambling. All these are rational considerations.

The example of legalized abortion

Let's consider perhaps the most controversial of all decisions made in courts and legislatures. Should abortion be permitted on demand, curbed, made illegal, or made legal in some cases and not others? Should it be illegal a certain number of months after conception? How will legislators decide the matter? How will voters decide what importance to attach to the issue?

Some will consider the woman's right to control her own body as the primary issue. Some will argue that since all the functions of life are present in the fetus, the fetus is a human life, and therefore abortion is murder. Some will look at the potential damage to society that comes from unrestricted abortion. They may argue that destroying a fetus makes it easier later on to kill the aged. Others may argue that easy abortion laws contribute to an irresponsible attitude about life and morality in general.

One common denominator is present in all the considerations going into the decision: reason. The answer that *appears to be most reasonable*, whether in the ballot box or in the legislative body, will determine that person's vote.

The problem with reason

There is a fundamental problem with human reason, however. That problem affects and infects all the choices people make based on human reason alone. The problem is sin.

Tragically, Adam and Eve lost the image of God when they fell into sin. Read the saddest story ever told. It is recorded in Genesis 3. As a result of the fall, the whole human race lost the image of God.

Some aspects of that image were lost completely. The essence of God's image was perfect holiness and righteousness. Adam and Eve's sin meant holiness and righteousness were completely destroyed. One cannot be a little bit holy and a little bit sinful; a person is either one or the other. Having lost holiness and righteousness, they could not bring forth holy and righteous children. "In Adam's fall, we sinned all," an old primer says.

The only way to get back that most important part of the image of God is by an act of God. We cannot contribute or help to get it back. God gives it back when he forgives our sin because of the work of Christ. The holiness and righteousness, yes, the sinlessness, that we have now are not ours by nature or by our efforts and works or because we figured out how to get them back with our reason. They are ours solely because God forgives us, because Christ took our sin on himself. He keeps on giving us that holiness and righteousness in the proclamation of the gospel.

What about Adam and Eve's ability to think, to use reason, after the fall? Again, read Genesis 3. You will see at once what has happened to human reason. Sin did not only destroy holiness and righteousness. Sin also corrupted and tragically damaged the ability to reason properly.

Adam and Eve became afraid of God, so they hid from him in the garden. That seemed reasonable to them, but in fact it was very unreasonable. God is everywhere; we cannot hide from him. Adam and Eve should have known that. Nevertheless, they ignored what they knew and took a course of action that only *seemed* reasonable.

Adam did not answer God's questions with a confession. In his fear he pointed the finger of blame. That seemed to him the most reasonable course of action. Eve did the same thing. Of course, since God knows everything, that course of action was not reasonable; it only seemed so.

Do you begin to see the problem with human reason? Since the fall, reason is totally corrupted in spiritual things; that is, human reason cannot bring us to faith; it cannot bring us to a true love of God; it cannot save us from sin, death, and hell. Again, only the gospel can do those things. Spiritually we are dead in trespasses and sins. That is our condition by nature, from the moment of conception (Ephesians 2:1-5).

To be sure, God left human beings with minds and the ability to think *some* things through. Even after the fall, people could use reason profitably. God subjected to human reason the things of this world—*not* spiritual things like faith in Christ and perfect love for God and one another. With reason we can figure out how to build a fire, fly an airplane, and drive a car. With reason we can figure out the best way to get from one place to

another. With reason we can make job, family, and retire-
ment decisions. God has left nonspiritual things to
human reason.

God even has left us with the ability to make some
outward moral choices with our reason. For example, a
person may decide not to murder, steal, or commit adul-
tery. A person may decide to lead an outwardly decent
and respectable life. A person may even decide to devote
his or her life to helping humanity, to making the world a
better place. People's reasoning powers may give a high
degree of understanding about what is best for themselves
and their country.

To put it another way, a person's grasp of natural law
may be very highly developed. One may with the natural
law and reason come close to the *outward behavior* required
in the Fourth to Tenth Commandments. But no one can
decide to do any of these things out of perfect love for
God and trust in his mercy. That's a spiritual ability, and
that ability is gone. Only the gospel can restore it.

When people without the gospel decide with their reason to lead honorable lives, they do it for reasons of their
own. They may conclude that such lives are more peaceful
than the lives of the undisciplined. Therefore it makes
sense to curb hate and lust and greed.

Some may conclude that outwardly moral lives are
good for society and therefore ultimately best also for self.
That's a rational decision. Others may conclude that they
want the respect of their neighbors and the honor of the
nation. With those as their rational motives, such people
even may do great heroic deeds, and by those deeds they
may win the well-deserved praise of a grateful nation.

So reason did not die as a result of the fall except in
the most important matters of all, matters of faith. In mat-

ters of this world, even in matters of outward morality, human reason functions and is active.

There is still a problem, however: sin. Sin has so completely infected our nature that our reason, even though it *can* function in nonspiritual things, often fails to function properly. Often when people try to make rational decisions, they reason poorly.

They may not give proper weight to what is really important. They may confuse what they *want* with what is *rational* and think the two are the same thing. Who of us has not experienced that? We decide we *want* a new car; then we look for a reason—we try to explain why we *need* a new car! Or we let our reason be overruled by our emotions and affections. Reason tells us one piece of chocolate cake is enough. Affections overrule, and we have another piece. Reason and natural law and conscience all may combine to tell an adulterer that he or she is heading for ruin, but emotion and passion overrule.

The examples of the school board vote on curriculum, the gambling debate, and the battle over abortion illustrate the point. Each person uses reason to make a political and a moral choice. Some give too much weight to unimportant considerations. Some bend their reason to suit their own personal interests: What's right or wrong is not important; getting reelected is, and so is justifying one's own behavior.

Thus even in those things God has left for us to decide on the basis of reason, people very often make wrong choices. Their reasoning is flawed or corrupted by selfishness, greed, or lust for power. They miss or ignore or corrupt even much of what they should be able to figure out on the basis of natural law written in the heart, just as Paul said in Romans 1.

It's a wonder society and government survive at all! Indeed, only because of God's rule over history and his mercy toward all people does society survive. When a society or a state collapses, it does so under the weight of decisions made that seemed rational but were in fact wicked, or it collapses because the state and society acted contrary even to their own best use of reason.

To sum up this very important point:

1. Human reason is by nature dead to the true love of God and trust in God; such things come only from the Holy Spirit working through God's Word.

2. Human reason is not dead in purely physical or natural things. People can make rational decisions about their lives in this world on the basis of the facts they possess; they can figure out physical and natural things logically.

3. Even in matters of *outward* morality, people can make rational and logical choices. They can decide whether to lead outwardly good and noble lives with reason.

4. The fact that people *can* make reasonable moral choices does not mean they always *do* make reasonable moral choices.

Fallen reason and government

Is it perhaps a little easier now to see why political choices are so difficult for people? Sometimes people make good rational choices. Sometimes people make choices that only seem rational. Sometimes people make choices in which reason has been thrown out of consideration all together. Their reason may have been blinded by self-interest, greed, a desire for revenge, or a whole host of other sinful traits. Rarely can anyone say with certainty, This is the right and only rational thing to do!

Should government cut back on welfare? Should government expand welfare? The arguments marshaled on each side may appear rational to the supporters of that side. But both sides cannot be right. The two sides may decide to compromise. That may be the most rational choice, not because each has agreed the other has a valid point but because the alternative is deadlock. Even then some on each side will insist deadlock is better than compromise and make a rational case for that position too.

That's the way government makes decisions. Leaders marshal facts. Some facts may be ignored. The importance of other facts may be exaggerated. In the interest of winning, some will lie and deceive. In the interest of personal advantage, others will attack their opponents' reputations, even though that has nothing to do with the question to be decided. Still others will honorably seek the facts and try as best they can to make a decision that is in the best interests of all or most.

Christians' advantage

In the whole maze of political arguments and decision making, Christians have one enormous advantage. Their reasoning is guided by the unerring Word of God. As the psalmist prays, "Your word is a lamp to my feet and a light for my path" (Psalm 119:105). Christians do not need to figure out moral principles or natural law all by themselves. We have the revealed law of God in the Bible.

Since the Word of God is without error, most moral issues are clearly decided for Christians by the Word of God. From the Word of God, Christians *know* what is right and wrong. Christians do not have to figure that out with their fallen reason, because God knows all things and weighs all things rightly. God's reasoning is without error or flaw of any kind. Therefore Christians most gladly yield to God's Word and subject reason to the mind of God in the Bible.

God's Word tells the Christian how the world began in Genesis 1 and 2. That settles the matter. God's Word tells the Christian that the sexual union is only for a husband and a wife in marriage. A Christian knows that such a union outside marriage is a sin. That ends arguments about the rights and wrongs of homosexuality and "trial marriages." The Christian knows from the Word of God that life begins at conception. That settles most arguments about abortion. (The only argument remaining is, What should we do if the life of the mother is seriously at risk? In which case we have to decide which life to protect.)

Countless other issues are settled for Christians by the Word of God. God's reasoning is always perfect. If it does not mesh with ours, then our reasoning is flawed and mistaken. We may not see clearly what the mistake is in our reasoning, but that does not matter. God is always right. Human beings, even with the best use of reason, can be and often are mistaken.

Clearly Christians have an enormous advantage over those who must figure everything out with only their corrupted reason as a guide. What a blessing Christians can be for a state! They can support positions they *know* are God-pleasing because God has decided the issue in his Word.

Difficult choices

Of course, not all issues will be so clear for Christians. We may have to choose between political candidates whose positions are sometimes correct but other times incorrect. For example, Candidate A opposes abortion on demand but also insists schools teach only evolution or perhaps favors a bill that would legalize homosexual marriages. Candidate B has the opposite position on each of those issues. Christians will sometimes have difficulty deciding which issues are most important.

We will weigh the potential for damage and for good as we try to make the best choice possible. We will pray for God's blessing as we wrestle with difficult choices. We do not expect God to whisper a choice in our ears, however. He has left the choice to us. God speaks in his Word and has never promised to speak apart from it, which is all the more reason, then, that Christians should be as well informed as possible about candidates and issues.

At other times Christians are confronted with still more difficult choices. For example, Candidate A is willing to compromise on some moral issues, perhaps on abortion. Candidate B is completely opposed to any limits on abortion. What should we do? Should we refuse to vote and thus help Candidate B? Or should we swallow hard and vote for Candidate A as the best of a flawed lot of alternatives? Perhaps Candidate A is swallowing hard too, knowing that his or her position is as far as the electorate will go and that it is still better than the opponent's position. Again, the individual Christian must wrestle with the issues and the choices at hand. A perfect solution to the problem may not be possible.

Other issues come up where a choice is not clearly made for us by the Word of God. Should the bond issue be passed for the new school? Should taxes be lowered so that people can spend more of their own money as they think best? Should taxes be raised so that society can do a better job of helping those who cannot help themselves? Do we really need a new water system, a new program for veterans, affirmative action to advance minorities, more police, more prisons, more laws against illegal immigration?

In making choices where God's Word does not obviously settle the matter, what do we do? We remember Paul's words: "As we have opportunity, let us do good to all people, especially to those who belong to the family of believers" (Galatians 6:10). Our goal is to serve our neighbor. As we decide things not settled by the Word of God, we keep that principle uppermost in our minds and hearts.

To be sure, in such cases we may not always agree with one another. One Christian may decide that one position best serves our neighbor, and a fellow Christian may conclude the opposite. But where God's Word has not decided the issue, the two can agree to disagree.

No apparent choices?

What if Christians find that the choices for political leaders are hopelessly flawed? What if they have concluded that all in the running are wrong on major issues clearly decided by the Word of God. What then?

Sometimes Christians with no honorable alternatives may have no choice but to leave the political decisions to others. We may have little we can do besides pray for the state and pray that better choices will emerge somehow. But we might also look around for just such better candidates and choices. We might encourage others who have the ability to run for office.

Perhaps *you* could run for office! Perhaps *you* are the one others are seeking out as a better choice! Is there a better way to serve the state? Is there a more important way to show love to our neighbor than to serve as an official of the state and carry out the office with honor and Christian morality?

Christian leaders are always in short supply. How blessed the land where their numbers increase! To be sure, sometimes the short supply of Christian leaders is the result of rejection; the majority voted against them. But how often are there no Christian leaders because none stepped forward?

The problem for Christians in the political arena

Christians can indeed be a great blessing to society and the state. Even those who do not become political candidates themselves are still a blessing to the state in the kinds of political choices they make as Christians guided by the Word of God. But a word of caution is in place: In all things political, we need to keep in mind the important principle mentioned earlier: *The state runs on the gasoline of human reason and natural law, not on the water of life in God's Word!* God has not given his Word to government, the earthly kingdom; he has given it to the church.

Christians who take a political position or run for a political office should keep this principle in mind. It should not be the business of Christians to become preachers of the gospel in politics. When we take a position in a public political debate, it serves no purpose to declare, "This is what the Word of the Lord says!"

That may sound shocking, but it is true. The state is not the church. The state runs on reason, not on the Word and the sacraments. There is no such thing as a Christian state, in spite of numerous attempts to create one. God, as we have seen, has given different responsibilities and tools to church and state. Christians who enter the political arena in order to establish Christian govern-ment confuse the two kingdoms in a way that will prove harmful to both.

How, then, does a Christian stay a Christian when serving or voting or campaigning in the political arena?

The connection between religious and political convictions

Christians' convictions are formed by the Word of God as proclaimed in church. Those convictions do not change when Christians consider political questions. But the way in which Christians defend their convictions in a political arena does change.

In discussing our religious beliefs, it is sufficient to say: "This is what the Bible says, and that is all I need to know. The Bible says that murder is a sin, and therefore I oppose abortion on demand." But when we translate that convic-tion formed by the Word of God into a political position argued in a political forum, human reason is the basis for the discussion. To enter a political forum with the lan-guage of the Word of God would be as sensible as speaking in Latin at the meeting. The Word of God simply is not the language of the discussion. Reason is.

Thus when opposing abortion in a political arena or as a candidate, we might present arguments like this: "Medi-cal science shows that a fetus is not mere tissue but a developing human being. Both an unborn fetus and a just-born child are totally dependent on others for life. The only real difference between the two is one of location and the manner of feeding. Therefore arguing that to kill the one is not murder and to kill the other is murder is unrea-sonable. Besides that, the introduction of abortion on demand hardens society's appreciation for life at any age or stage. In the interests of the old and the weak, we need to defend life at every stage."

That is by no means a complete argument, but hopefully the point is made. A Christian conviction formed by the Word of God can be argued in a political forum on a rational basis.

The same is true in the example of a school board debate over curriculum. It is enough for the Christian as a Christian to say: "The Bible teaches a six-day creation; therefore I cannot accept the theory of evolution. The Bible tells us what life is, what a family is, and what duties we owe to one another in the family; therefore that family-life curriculum is wrong and this family-life curriculum is better." But when the debate occurs before the school board, what satisfies us as Christians because God's Word says so is not enough. Someone will quickly respond to the answer from the Bible: "This is not the church. Nor is it the business of the public school to teach what your church teaches or what the Bible teaches."

The one who answered thus will be right. The school board is guided not by the Bible but by human reason. A Christian, however, might call up a number of arguments on the basis of reason to make his or her points. A Christian might argue, for example: "It is true; the public school is not in the business of imposing what the Bible says on anyone. However, it also has no right to impose on my children beliefs contrary to the Bible. Therefore at the very least I should expect respect for the right to my beliefs. And let me point out that these convictions are not wild or extreme but shared by millions for centuries. In a society that claims to be democratic, our views also deserve respectful hearing."

Again, that argument is by no means complete. The point is that the debate in the political arena is carried out on the basis of reason, even though our own convictions have first been formed by the Word of God. There is nothing wrong with a Christian arguing in the political arena on the basis of reason even though his or her reason has first been taken captive by the Word of God. No reasoning in the world is more solid and sound than reasoning that submits to the Word of God, who alone is all wise!

8

Soldiers, War, and Courts

In Chapter 7 we considered some ways in which a Christian may act as a citizen in the service of the state. In this chapter we will consider the issues of a Christian serving as a soldier in the armed forces, participating in wars, and making use of civil courts.

Christians as soldiers

It is not a sin to be a soldier. The New Testament makes that clear a number of times. When the soldiers came to John the Baptist to ask him what they should do as a fruit of repentance, he said, "Don't extort money and don't accuse people falsely—be content with your pay" (Luke 3:14). John did not tell them to find a way to get out of the army. He told them to conduct themselves honorably and according to the moral law.

To be sure, soldiers may have to take human life in the course of their service. But they act then not as private citizens. They act as the instrument of the state, to whom God has given the sword (Romans 13:4). In carrying out their duty, soldiers are not guilty of murder. Otherwise John would have had to command the soldiers who came to him to leave the army, because their very occupation would have been a sin, since it carries with it the possibility of taking a life. The same would hold true for those on the police force.

Jesus also came into contact with believing soldiers. Jesus healed the servant of a centurion, a Roman military officer, and even praised the faith of that centurion (Luke 7:9). If serving in the army were in itself a faith-destroying sin, Jesus could not have spoken of the centurion as he did.

Finally, one of the most interesting stories in the book of Acts takes place in the home of a soldier. The apostle Peter went to the home of the centurion Cornelius and preached the gospel. The Holy Spirit worked faith through that preaching of the gospel (Acts 10). In the whole of the account, there is nothing to suggest that Cornelius should change his occupation. Cornelius was converted as a soldier and, as far as we know, continued to live as a soldier.

Just and unjust wars

The issues we have discussed in the previous chapter and thus far in this chapter are primarily issues of local politics and personal matters. But one problem Christians have confronted down through the ages is clearly and always national in its scope: war.

Jesus told us there would be wars (Matthew 24:6,7), and no age of history has been without them. Some wars are defensive. The nation is attacked. The leaders call the citizens to arms. To refuse to go and defend one's country is a crime against the state and a sin as well. We have no greater outward duty toward our neighbors than to help and defend them, as Luther points out in the Small Catechism under the Fifth Commandment. Wars of defense do not present Christians with a problem.

But what about offensive wars? What about wars in which the Christian's own nation is under no direct attack and in no immediate danger? In some such wars a nation may be going to the defense of an ally. The leaders may argue that to refuse help to a friendly nation can only mean a worse war later on. Or the leaders may argue that the nation has a moral obligation to defend the ally according to some treaty. At times a country will wage an offensive war to punish great evil. Humanity cries out for the defense of a population suffering intolerably at the hands of its own rulers. Even in ancient times, countries looked for ways to save a neighboring country from a monster. The example of Count Vlad the Impaler comes to mind. He turned his whole country into a torture chamber, and neighboring princes were so horrified that they looked for ways of overthrowing him. Examples of such wars are rare.

Generally speaking, these two kinds of offensive wars also have been called just wars. Christians may sometimes be suspicious of leaders who want to wage such offensive wars, however. Indeed, Christians may differ among themselves about whether a particular war is just: Is the reason given for going to war really a cover for greed, lust for power, or a nationalistic ambition for domination?

Especially in the 20th century, the consciences of many Christians have been deeply troubled by the problem of unjust war. War has never been more cruel or bloody. Bombs do not just destroy factories and armaments plants. They burn, maim, and kill innocent men, women, and children. They destroy the lives of those who are in no way to blame for the war on a scale inconceivable before the 20th century.

What a terrible thing it must be in the eyes of God to cause an unjust war, a war waged only out of greed or lust for power! What a monstrous thing in an unjust war to shed the blood of the innocent and to inflict unspeakable suffering on those who survive!

Christians as conscientious objectors

Must Christians fight in a war they consider unjust? No! The goal of the Christian life is service to God by service to our neighbor. To fight in an unjust war renders no service to God or to one's neighbor. It serves only the greed and the ambition of those who want others to bleed and die for the sake of selfish gain.

Before Christians could refuse to serve in the armed forces, however, they would have to be convinced by evidence that the war is indeed unjust. If there is clear and convincing proof of that, they should refuse to fight. They also will have to be prepared to take the consequences of such a refusal. They might have to flee the country. If they stay, they may endure imprisonment or worse. Rebellion and revolution are not options. They are always contrary to the Word of God.

Many countries recognize what is called conscientious objector status. That is, those who claim it would be against their consciences to fight in a war may be granted some kind of exemption from military service; some countries offer alternative community service. Christians must be very careful in claiming such a status. They must be very sure that the war is indeed an unjust war. If there is room for doubt, the benefit of the doubt goes to one's leaders. Luther in his explanation to the Eighth Commandment reminds us that we should think the best of other people's motives and intentions. That applies to our government as well. If it turns out that our leaders lied and deceived, the guilt and blame is theirs, not ours. The blood is on their heads and hands. That may be cold comfort indeed to one whose nights are disturbed by dreams of war and of blood shed for unjust ends.

Soldiers plagued by feelings of guilt need to flee to the gospel for help; that is true even when the guilt really belongs to those who deceived them. Sometimes the Christian's greatest battle is not with temptations to obvious sins; it is rather with temptations within, temptations to doubt and despair. That can be the case even when the sense of guilt is not entirely justified. The gospel in Word and sacrament remains the only cure, the only comfort.

When it comes to deciding whether a war is just or unjust, the individual citizen, Christian or not, has a very difficult time. The propaganda organs of the state are well oiled and armed so that the enemy is made to appear inhuman. Often the country finds out the true nature of the conflict only long after the damage is done. Thus we do the best we can with the information we have. We beg God to spare us from war and bloodshed. But if human wickedness spoils God's designs for peace, Christians too must fight to defend their homeland.

Christians and the courts

As citizens of our nation, we are, of course, subject to the laws of the land. That means we are subject also to its court system.

Clearly, Christians will not want to take advantage of the law and the courts to accomplish greedy or otherwise evil ends. Luther in the Small Catechism warns us against trying to gain our neighbor's property by a "show of right." He warns us not to go to court with the mere appearance of a legal right, when we know perfectly well we have no moral right.

Many battles in court over contested wills are nothing more than evidence of coveting and greed. The same might be said over lawsuits in many accident cases, contract disputes, property fights, and the like.

Someone who is both in the world and of the world using the courts in such a way need not surprise us. But Christians using the courts in the same manner shocked the apostle Paul and should shock us too! What a contradiction to our profession that we are in the world but not of it. In 1 Corinthians 6:1-8, Paul urged the Christians in Corinth not to go before unbelievers for judgment:

> If any of you has a dispute with another, dare he take it before the ungodly for judgment instead of before the saints? Do you not know that the saints will judge the world? And if you are to judge the world, are you not competent to judge trivial cases? Do you not know that we will judge angels? How much more the things of this life! Therefore, if you have disputes about such matters, appoint as judges even men of little account in the church! I say this to shame you. Is it possible that there is nobody among you wise enough to judge a dispute between believers? But instead, one brother goes to law against another—and this in front of unbelievers! The very fact that you have law-

suits among you means you have been completely defeated already. Why not rather be wronged? Why not rather be cheated? Instead, you yourselves cheat and do wrong, and you do this to your brothers.

Christians should be able to solve their disputes among themselves, Paul pointed out. He also urged them to avoid lawsuits against each other altogether. Christians should suffer wrong rather than give the appearance of being greedy heathens.

In the Sermon on the Mount, Jesus too warns against greed and selfishness. He does that in the context of legal rights; he tells us we should even endure injustice if we can serve our neighbor thereby (Matthew 5:38-48).

Notice again how consistent the Bible is when it speaks of our lives as citizens of the earthly kingdom. The goal always remains the same: Showing obedience and love to God by serving our neighbor. That way we bring honor to Christ our King; that way we serve the cause of the gospel by the witness of a Christian life.

When may Christians go to court?

Does showing obedience and love to God by serving our neighbor mean Christians may never go to court? Does it mean they should never resist if they are sued? Does it mean they should never sue if they have been wronged? Does it mean they should forego the legal rights and privileges we have as citizens of the land?

The personal example of the apostle Paul shows that Christians too can make use of the courts for their defense against blatant injustice. In the city of Philippi, Paul was unjustly accused and imprisoned and illegally beaten. The next day, when the court wanted to release

Paul, he took advantage of his rights as a Roman citizen. He insisted that the court demonstrate to the public his innocence of any crime. He would not leave the prison until the officials themselves came and escorted him out (Acts 16:22-40).

Paul did not want the public to think he was guilty of crime or rebellion. If he had quietly left town, just such a wrong impression could have been left behind. What law-abiding citizen would want to hear the gospel if its great messenger was thought to be a rebel and an evildoer?

At the close of the book of Acts, Paul again made full use of his legal rights. He defended himself against unjust accusations. When he clearly could not get a fair trial, he used his right as a Roman citizen to appeal his case to the emperor (Acts 21:27–26:32).

There is no contradiction between Paul's words in 1 Corinthians and the way he made use of his civil rights, as described in the book of Acts. Christians may make use of the legal system to protect themselves against injustice.

This right is maintained in the Lutheran Confessions. The Formula of Concord says a Christian "may use an office of the government against wicked people" without violating his conscience.[2] According to the Apology of the Augsburg Confession, private revenge is forbidden, but "public redress through a judge is not forbidden but expressly commanded, and it is a work of God according to Paul (Rom. 13:1ff.)."[3]

When we do seek public redress, we need to remember Jesus' words in the Sermon on the Mount and Paul's warning in 1 Corinthians. There is a narrow middle road between use and misuse when protecting our rights. We all know how easy it is in our fallen nature to minimize our own wrongs and exaggerate the wrongs of our neighbor. In our society people all too often use the court system to avenge themselves on their enemies. We know too how easy it is for greed to find its way into our hearts. The temptation to try and get something we really have not earned by use of the courts is ever with us in our society.

The following questions may help Christians examine their hearts when considering court action: Is the right I want to exercise in court the rotten fruit of vengeance or greed? Will my legal action display a covetous heart? Or is it necessary for the defense of another and the protection of my family to make use of the legal remedies granted by the state?

Let's say Fred and Frieda were violently attacked and robbed. The criminals were caught. Should Fred and Frieda testify against them in court? Should Fred and Frieda seek restitution, perhaps even punitive damages from the criminals?

Fred and Frieda do not want vengeance. They want the evildoers to repent, even to hear the gospel and be converted. (Fred and Frieda are very fine Christians indeed!) But if they do not testify in court, the criminals will be released and free to harm others. Love for their neighbors compels Fred and Frieda to testify.

The same love for others might impel them to seek damages. If the criminals do not make restitution, Fred and Frieda's children will have to pay for the medical expenses and make good some other losses as well. On the other hand, if Fred and Frieda went to court merely to extract vengeance and get even, then Jesus' warning in Matthew 5 would certainly apply to them.

The point is that in each action we always need to examine our hearts, our motives. And that is nowhere more true than when we are considering legal action.

On occasion Christians may even be in the position of having to sue one another. That occurs sometimes in a "friendly lawsuit"; an insurance company may require a lawsuit in an accident claim before it will make a payment.

At other times the lawsuit may not be so friendly. Someone has taken advantage; someone has cheated a fellow believer; someone's legal rights are in doubt, and the doubt can only be removed by a court case. This is a precarious situation with the possibility for great offense. Paul told the believers in Corinth not to take other believers into a secular court. Yet it may be that someone who claims to be a Christian has really showed himself or herself to be an unbeliever by such actions. Certainly in this case, let a Christian proceed with fear and trembling!

No simple rule that covers every possible legal situation can be given, but the principle is the same as elsewhere: We live to serve him who loved us and gave himself for us; we would rather be deprived of rights and wealth, of life itself, than bring dishonor to him and to his Word.

Oaths

We have been considering the Christian as a citizen with legal rights and responsibilities. That raises for us the question of taking an oath to tell the truth, which we may be asked to do in a court case and often are asked to do on legal documents, such as contracts, deeds, and tax declarations.

When we take an oath, we publicly declare, either in writing or with spoken words, that we are telling the truth. On occasion we may even be asked to add the weighty words "So help me God!"

Some religious groups teach that taking oaths is a sin. They quote from Jesus' Sermon on the Mount (Matthew 5:33-37). Jesus says in these verses that we should not swear, that our yes and no should be enough, but he is not talking about courtrooms and governmental regulations. He is talking about the everyday life with one's neighbor.

Jesus' point is simply this: We should be known for our honesty and truthfulness. Therefore, because everyone knows we would not lie or deceive, it should not be necessary for us to take an oath, to swear we are telling the truth, in ordinary, everyday, trivial matters.

Clearly Jesus' words, as well as the Second and Eighth Commandments, forbid foolish oaths and telling a lie under oath. "I swear to God" should not be a Christian's exclamation point at the end of a sentence. But the Bible does not forbid taking oaths in all situations and circumstances. In court and on legal documents, we are not interacting with those who know us for our honesty. We are dealing with governmental regulations and official records of some importance or the possible punishment of someone else in a court case. Jesus himself was called on to take an oath in court, and he took it (Matthew 26:63,64).

It should be obvious that to lie under oath is a sin. How terrible it was for Peter that he denied his Lord. How even more shameful it was that he tried to cover up his lie by calling on God's name in an oath (Matthew 26:69-75).

In this entire consideration of the Christian as a citizen, the reader may notice that the emphasis throughout has been more on responsibilities than on rights. That emphasis will clearly mark a Christian as different from many others in the land.

Service to God and service to our neighbor that flows from love to God and loyalty to his Word—those hallmarks of the Christian life will often mean we even give up rights in the interest of responsibility, of service.

In conclusion

As Christians we carry out our duties to the state. We work faithfully in our respective jobs. We pay taxes honestly. We pray for the state. We vote in elections. We support candidates. We champion various political causes and take sides in political debates. We may even run for office ourselves. We fight in our country's wars. At times we make use of our legal rights in court. We do all these things and more out of love to God and in service to our neighbor. We live in the world, even though we are not of it.

In our service to the state, the other kingdom, we have no illusions. We know our best efforts in serving will not always be appreciated. We know we will not always be on the winning side of a moral issue but usually in the minority. That awareness should not deter us, however. It is not an excuse to give up. It is an incentive to remember that God has called us to be faithful.

We are content to leave the results in the Lord's hands. After all, he is Christ the King. His rule is over all the earth. Ultimately his will is done. On judgment day his reign will be obvious to all. We are not at judgment day yet, though surely it is drawing near. Therefore let us serve Christ the King with faithfulness to his Word. Let us serve the state and thereby our neighbor because it pleases Christ the King. Let us do that as we do all things, trusting in his mercy and waiting for his salvation.

Part II

The History
of Church-State Relations

9

From the Apostles to Constantine

In Chapters 6 to 8 our concern was an individual Christian's relationship with the state. But Christians also join together. They want and need the fellowship of other Christians. No one can carry out the Great Commission (Matthew 18:18-20) alone. Christians, therefore, form churches and federations; they build schools and hospitals; they organize societies for missions, for education, for the support of those in need.

When Christians combine to form a church or church-related organization, the problem of church-state relations becomes much more involved and complicated. In this chapter and the next, we want to consider the history of church-state relations from the time of the apostles to the time of the Reformation. The history will show us how important it is to remember what God has said about the distinct roles of church and state. The history will also show us what happens when church and state forget their God-assigned works and roles.

Persecution

The history of contact between church and state from the time of the apostles until about A.D. 315 can be summed up in one word: persecution!

During most of this period, the Christian religion was illegal. The church did not have fine buildings. There were no beautiful school buildings, colleges, or seminaries. Services often were conducted in secret. Christians shared their faith with unbelievers at great personal risk.

Why was the church persecuted?

In the history of governments, there has been a common theme when it comes to religion. We see it played out in the Old Testament. We discover it again and again in one empire after another. The theme is this: Religion can be a useful tool of the state for uniting a divided nation.

That is undoubtedly what was at the bottom of Nebuchadnezzar's scheme recorded in Daniel 3. He ruled over an empire of many peoples and religions. One way to tie the empire together would be the establishment of a common religion. Nebuchadnezzar did not care that people worshiped other gods. They could worship as many as they liked. But among the gods they served, one god would tie them together with everyone else in the empire: Nebuchadnezzar's golden image. The three Hebrews got into trouble because they refused to worship any god other than the true God.

Emperor worship

By New Testament times, government use of religion as a unifying factor was already an old habit. Very often the state decreed that the ruler himself was a god. In ancient Egypt the pharaoh was thought by the people to be a descendant of the gods. The same was true in the Roman Empire; it became common to speak of the emperor as the son of God. Sometimes emperors were declared to be gods by the Roman Senate after their death.

It did not really make much difference to the government whether one took the notion of a divine emperor seriously. But it made a great deal of difference when someone refused to perform the public ritual of burning incense to the emperor. Refusal to go along publicly with the ritual worship of the emperor was seen by the government as treason. The reasoning went this way: Those who worship the emperor will not participate in a revolt against him; those who refuse even to burn a pinch of incense before his image simply are not to be trusted—they could revolt!

From the time of the apostles until shortly after A.D. 300, the Roman Empire went through one crisis after another. In fact, the empire was dying. The weaker the empire became, the more important the practice of emperor worship became. The government wanted to use it as a sort of glue to hold together the state, which was falling apart.

A growing church brought increased persecution

Christianity grew rapidly during this entire period. The more it grew, the more frightened the state became, because the Christians refused to worship the emperor. The government's fear had much to do with the social status of Christians. Many converts were from the lowest classes; they were people who were overtaxed and underserved by government. Many were slaves. A large number of soldiers also became Christians. The very fact that slaves and soldiers were becoming Christians in such large numbers made the government especially nervous. The state always feared a slave revolt and also was afraid that Christians in the army might not be reliable in defense of the state or might even overthrow it.

Beginning with the apostles, therefore, persecution of Christianity was a common theme of church-state relations. But as the early church fathers pointed out, the state had nothing to fear from the church, because the Christians were taught to obey the state and respect its authority. In fact, the church fathers said, it was not the Christians who were a threat to the state. Quite the contrary, the immorality of the heathen was undermining its stability.

The defense of the church by her teachers accomplished little. Persecutions continued, sometimes locally, sometimes throughout the empire. But persecution did not accomplish the purposes of the state either. The Christians continued refusing to worship the emperor, and Christianity spread in spite of persecution.

The nature of the persecution

We must admire the faithfulness of those early Christians, beginning with the apostles. All the apostles died martyrs' deaths, according to tradition, except John, who died on a prison island. Other Christians suffered too. Children of Christians were taken away and sold into slavery; if they were too young to be sold, they were taken into the forest and left to die. Adults were sent to salt mines or to work as oarsmen on galley ships; they died in slavery.

Others were sent to provide entertainment in the arena; they were killed by gladiators' swords or by the mouths of wild animals. But they did not revolt!

It made no difference whether the church had many members or few; it made no difference how many were in the army; it made no difference how severe the persecution became: Christians did not revolt!

In some places the government rewarded anyone who turned in a Christian. The spy was given part or all of the Christian's property. At the Christian's trial, only one question was asked: Will you burn incense to the emperor? If the accused refused, that was enough to prove he or she belonged to an illegal religion; that was enough to condemn him or her to loss of property, slavery, or death.

In spite of persecution

The faith of the church lived on in spite of persecution. Pastors were trained by other pastors. Christians shared their faith in dangerous circumstances. The church grew. The New Testament Scriptures were copied and circulated. The Apostles' Creed was developed as the common confession of the church, especially at Baptism. The Sacrament of the Altar was celebrated. (In fact, the Sacrament of the Altar became a common excuse for persecuting Christians: Christians teach that Christ's body and blood are really present in the Sacrament; therefore, said the pagans, Christians are cannibals.) Through all this Christ kept his promise that not even the gates of hell itself could destroy the church (Matthew 16:18).

The relations between church and state for these almost three hundred years were quite simple: the state persecuted, and the church endured persecution. The church still prayed *for* the state—just not *to* it.

Constantine

An important turning point came in history and in church-state relations in A.D. 312. A civil war of sorts was going on in the Roman army. Part of the army declared Constantine the Roman emperor in what today is Britain, France, and Spain. In Rome the emperor Maxentius was furious. He ruled the Roman Empire in Italy and North Africa and wanted control of the north and west as well.

To settle the matter, the army of Constantine marched towards Rome. The night before the decisive battle, Constantine thought he saw a sign in the sky above the setting sun: a cross with words around it, either "In this sign conquer!" or "In this sign you will conquer!" To Constantine it was an important omen: If he won with a cross emblazoned on his battle standards, then he would give credit for the victory to Christ.

Constantine's mother was a Christian. Some of his soldiers were as well. Constantine himself was not a Christian. But the next day in battle under the sign of the cross, he was completely victorious against overwhelming odds. As a result, Constantine was confirmed as emperor in the west.

He gave the credit for his victory to the God of the Christians and decided to become a Christian. But he delayed his baptism until his deathbed because he was afraid his sins after Baptism would not be forgiven. Nevertheless, he considered himself a Christian and a defender of the Christian religion.

The Edict of Milan

In A.D. 313 Constantine issued the famous Edict of Milan. In that decree he ordered that Christians should no longer be persecuted. The decree did not make Christianity the state religion; it granted freedom of conscience to non-Christians as well as to Christians.

In practice the decree of toleration opened the door to a climate of much more than mere toleration. Christianity soon and very obviously became the religion favored by the government. Large grants were given by the state for the building of churches. Tax exemptions and exemption from military service were given to pastors. The eagle, which had been the symbol of the empire, was replaced with a cross.

The favor of the state and of the emperor in particular caused a stampede of people into the church. Members of the upper classes, officials of government, and those who wanted or needed favor and business from the government all wanted to become Christians!

Sadly, many were insincere. Even more sadly, the church was poorly prepared to instruct these people. There simply were not enough trained pastors. What pastors there were could not keep up with the demands. Indeed, often the pastors were despised by those they were trying to teach. For these new "converts" were much better educated than the pastors. The church was overwhelmed.

There were many unhappy consequences of this sudden change from a persecuted church to a favored church. Superstition and saint worship began in earnest during this period. Pagans brought their favorite old gods with them and renamed them for some saint.

Worst of all, more and more Christians began to fall into work-righteousness. The battle against work-righteousness and self-righteousness is always a problem for the church. It was before Constantine's conversion too. But during this period the threat of work-righteousness inside the church grew rapidly.

Serious Christians, Christians who had lived through the persecutions, saw the immorality of the new "converts." They also saw people who had left during persecution come back to church. Sometimes those who returned—and sat next to them in church—were the same people who traitorously had turned in their relatives during the persecution.

Surely, these serious Christians thought, God does not forgive these heathen; surely he does not just forgive people who turned in our relatives and were responsible for their suffering and death! The terrible false doctrine that God's forgiveness and grace are limited, especially after Baptism, began to attack some of the best and most faithful members of the church.

Other serious doctrinal problems also came to the surface. A number of scholars had become Christians even before the time of Constantine. They argued about the nature of Christ's relationship with the Father. Was Christ *the same as* God, or was Christ merely *like* God? These doctrinal problems bothered Constantine. No doubt, his concern for the unity of the church was genuine. But his concern for the unity of the empire was at least as earnest.

Just as previous governments had used emperor worship as a glue for the empire, so Constantine and his successors expected Christianity to serve as the new glue! Doctrinal divisions would have to be resolved—*by the state* as well as the church.

The Council of Nicea

In order to settle the doctrinal divisions in the church, especially those concerning the person of Christ, Constantine summoned a church council and presided over it as well.

The goal was noble in many respects, and in many respects the results were of great benefit to the church. The hero of the council was Athanasius from Alexandria in Egypt. He was the main author of what we today call the Nicene Creed. The Council of Nicea and the Nicene Creed rejected the view that Christ is merely similar to God. It confessed the truth of the Scriptures that Christ is fully and truly God.

As important as the Nicene Creed was, however, the Council of Nicea set a bad precedent of government getting involved in the affairs of the church. God has not given even a Christian emperor the responsibility for establishing the faith of the church. That is not the task of the state, even if the ruler's faith is the correct one.

It did not take long for the council to show itself as a bad precedent. After the council had finished its work and adjourned, heretics gained influence over the emperor and his court. The ink was barely dry on the first draft of the Nicene Creed when the government threw it out, deciding in favor of the view that Christ is merely similar to God, not God from God.

Guess what happened—persecution! Athanasius was banished and exiled and in fact died before the Nicene Creed finally triumphed. Other faithful pastors met a similar fate.

The Nicene Creed's triumph by A.D. 385 was as much the work of the government as of the church.

After Constantine

Most of the emperors after Constantine were Christians. And most of them considered it their business to protect and promote the Christian religion at the point of a sword if need be. Even in territories where the Roman army was not in control, mission activity often was carried on at the point of a sword: The chief of a tribe was converted and saw to it that his people were converted too. If some refused Baptism in the river, they would drown in the river!

Whether the territory was under imperial control or not, government played an important role in the work and life of the church. Princes, kings, and emperors considered it their duty to protect and advance the faith of the church. That assumption may have been prompted by noble goals and pious hearts, but increasingly that assumption hurt both the church and the state.

The church in the east

As the Roman Empire continued its thousand-year decline, the government was moved out of Rome. Constantine had begun to build a new capital to the east of Greece, the great city of Constantinople.

Once the government was established in Constantinople, the emperors controlled the election of the bishops there. With control of the bishops came control over doctrine. An emperor, for example, would decide that images (sacred pictures) of Christ and the saints were bad. Therefore they were abolished, and those who had them were declared both heretics and criminals. The next emperor had the opposite view. The process was again set in motion: Those who opposed images were declared heretics and criminals.

The church in the east and her doctrine became captives of the state. The church was reduced to a department of the government. Christianity was the glue of empire. To oppose or resist the emperor was heresy, and heresy was a crime against the state, to be punished by the state.

Even in art the propaganda of Christianity as state glue was carried out. The imperial family was depicted as standing with Christ. The emperor himself was often painted in priestly robes.

The peril in the marriage of church and state

It is a miracle that the church survived! When the bishops are government appointees and the pastors are basically officials of the state, what happens to the church? What happens to the care of souls? What happens to the poor, who need the gospel? What happens to concern for pure doctrine out of love for Christ alone?

All suffer. The energy and attention devoted to pleasing rulers is energy and attention not devoted to preaching the gospel. People with legitimate complaints against the state see the church as the handmaiden of their oppressor. People with no political clout see the clergy as uninterested in their concerns and spiritual well-being.

Again, it is a miracle—and a surprise—that the church survived. There were still faithful pastors and teachers. There were even some great theologians and church fathers. There were devoted and dedicated laypeople. But alongside these were the disgusted. Many simply went through the motions of attendance at worship services to avoid trouble with the state. Many a conscience was seared by the disappearance of Christ the merciful; he was replaced by Christ the judge in the imperial court.

How many despaired? How many died in despair because the church was too busy with the state to bother with troubled souls? How many assumed that citizenship in the earthly realm equaled citizenship in heaven? How many never became Christians because outward obedience to the state was all the church seemed to care about? How many never understood the gospel because legal acceptance of the creed was all that was necessary, whether the creed was understood or not?

In the next chapter we will see how the tendency to mix church and state, begun under Constantine, only continued, bringing further problems for the church and spiritual decline.

10

From the Middle Ages to Luther

The Muslim conquest

In the seventh century, Islam began its long march of conquest in the east. Syria, Palestine, Egypt, and all of North Africa fell before the invading Islamic armies.

Christianity survived the conquest, but just barely. As territory was conquered by the Muslims, a new church-state relationship began. Often the Muslims did not openly persecute Christianity. But the Muslim governments had two ingenious ways of separating Christians from their church.

First, the Muslim governments often made the pastors responsible for order and for taxes in their neighborhoods.

Thus the pastors became policemen and tax collectors. As control tightened, it tightened under the fist of the clergy. As taxes were raised, they were collected by the pastors. One can easily imagine how long it would take for people to disappear from a church like that.

Second, sons of Christians were taken for an elite unit of the Muslim army. Those units were the first into battle and often suffered the heaviest casualties. But if they survived, they were given every advantage. They became rich and sometimes powerful. Parents were torn: If they did not want their sons to be in the elite divisions of the army, they could leave the church. On the other hand, if they wanted their sons to have the best, they could have it only by giving them up to service in a Muslim army.

Again, the church survived, but just barely. The connection with the state was disastrous for the church. There is very little left of Christianity east of Greece and in North Africa.

The virtual disappearance of the church in the areas conquered by the Muslims was also aided by the earlier connection between the church and the state. The loyalty of the people to the church had been weakened because of the political ties between the emperor and the bishops. That weakness was fully exploited by the Muslim conquerors.

In Rome

Meanwhile in the old capital, Rome, history took a very different turn. Once the government moved its headquarters to Constantinople, the bishop of Rome became the only significant leader in Italy. His leadership quickly became political as well as religious. Many of the bishops became heroes for their brave defense of the city, which had been abandoned by the emperor. When tribes from the north came down to attack the city, it was often the bishop who went out to meet them.

These strong bishops looked with concern on what was happening to the church in Constantinople. It troubled them that the church was so completely under the control of the state. They correctly considered it the business of the church to decide doctrinal matters on the basis of the Word of God. In hundreds of years of trying to figure out how the church could be free from domination by the state, the Roman bishops came up with a possible solution to the problem: The church could become a state!

That is basically how the papal states originated. The bishops of Rome began to carve out for themselves a slice of territory in the middle of Italy. The goal was for that slice to reach from west to east until Italy was cut in two, with the papal states in the middle. That way no ruler could ever gain complete control of Italy. With no ruler able to completely control Italy, no ruler would be able to completely dominate the church. Thus the church would be free to decide doctrinal matters without interference from the state.

The goal was certainly a good and noble one. But whenever the means are wrong, it is just a matter of time before the noble goal is lost. And that is exactly what happened. Much of the history of Europe before the Reformation has more to do with power struggles between church and state than with doctrinal purity.

Northern Europe
With the Muslim conquests in the east and a much-weakened imperial government in Constantinople, power in western Europe shifted from Italy to the north.

In A.D. 800 the Frankish conqueror who came to be known as Charlemagne (Carl the Great) made himself emperor of a basically new western empire, which came to be known as "The Holy Roman Empire of the German Nation." Charlemagne's rise ushered in a new chapter in church-state relations in the west.

Already the name itself tells us a dangerous confusion of church and state was at the heart of this new empire. How can an empire be holy? The church is holy, not the state. The gospel gives holiness, not the sword.

Charlemagne's empire was poorly defined. Its territory extended from parts of Italy through parts of modern-day France, Germany, Austria, and Switzerland. In the years after A.D. 800, the government's control extended as far as the army could reach and no farther. One factor in the empire's development from the time of Charlemagne to the Reformation was a constant: the importance of the church in the political equation.

We noted earlier that the bishops in Rome were concerned about the condition of the church in Constantinople. They did not want their church to become a political football of powerful rulers; they did not want to be dominated by the state. Unfortunately, the only way that they could think of for avoiding such domination was this: Let the church dominate the state so that the state cannot dominate the church. In the west there was a struggle by the church to gain control of the state.

It was a long and bitter struggle! Rarely was there any clear winner. For a time the church was on top. Then the state gained the upper hand. But each victory by one side was the prelude to a new struggle for control by the other side. We cannot here detail all of the chapters and scandals of that struggle. Perhaps the little that follows will give the reader some idea of how things went.

The Roman bishop became head of the whole western church; he became the pope. Emperors realized how important that position was. Therefore the emperors after Charlemagne insisted on the right to a voice in the election of the pope. Old and powerful Roman families likewise insisted on a voice. In fact, these families often treated the papal office as a family possession; one family fought another to get it and to keep it, using bribery and even murder for control of the church. Other high church offices also were seen as the possession of powerful families. Still other offices were bought and sold.

Emperors and princes also insisted on the right to nominate, if not appoint, bishops in their own territories. Popes, on the other hand, declared that no prince was a prince unless the pope said so and that no emperor was an emperor until he was crowned by the pope.

The battles for control became vicious. On one occasion a pope was elected only with great difficulty. The emperor locked up the electors in the middle of a hot summer in a room with no ventilation and stationed his troops with no sanitary facilities on the leaking roof of the building. The election process was considerably shortened.

For about 70 years, the popes were even held as virtual prisoners of the French kings. They were taken out of Rome and installed in a castle in France so the government could keep a watchful eye on them.

There was viciousness on the other side as well. A pope made a German emperor walk barefoot in the Alps in the wintertime to show repentance for having resisted him. Worse still, if rulers refused to obey the worldly decrees of the pope, the pope would declare that the prince's subjects no longer needed to obey the prince. If that did not bring the prince or emperor into line, the pope threatened to close all the churches in his territory. Those who died without the sacraments and priestly ministry of the church believed they would go to hell. The mere threat of such a papal action was often cnough to bring governments into line.

In order to support their demand for both religious and political power, the popes began to make the most blasphemous claims. They declared it was necessary for salvation to submit to them in all things spiritual and temporal.

They claimed their rulings on any subject, whether religious or secular, came from God. There was no need for proof from the Bible. The pope's word was good enough to create both doctrines and kings, to change doctrines and to unseat kings! With these claims the popes fulfilled Paul's prophecy in 2 Thessalonians 2:1-12 of the coming of the Antichrist.

Through all this the separate roles God had assigned to church and state became hopelessly confused. Even in the best of times, earthly rulers assumed it was their duty to defend the church and to punish her foes with the sword. Ruling families took control of monasteries and bishoprics. Then they fought with other families about the control of still other monasteries and bishoprics. Thus, for example, the rulers of Saxony and Brandenburg fought over which family should control the bishopric of Magdeburg, and the ruling house of Bavaria fought to keep control of the archbishopric of Cologne.

Political control of religious institutions was important because bishops and archbishops held important seats in the German and French parliaments. In fact, of the seven votes it took to elect the German emperor, three of the votes were held by archbishops. It is easy to see why the struggle to control those positions became so intense.

Those within the church equally assumed that the church had political responsibilities, which even included the right of bishops to be worldly princes. Some of the largest principalities in Europe belonged not to political kings and princes, but to bishops and archbishops. The pope himself was not only the religious leader of the papal states; he was also the temporal ruler of that territory.

As nation states developed, the politics of the church became all the more complicated and intricate. The pope sided with the German emperor if the king of France grew too strong. He sided with the king of France if the German emperor grew too strong. The Spanish kingdoms also played into the equation, as did Portugal and some of the Italian city states.

Keep in mind what the original purpose of the church had been when it entered the political arena: to keep the church free from domination by the state. The church was anxious to be free from such domination so that the state could not dictate doctrine. But look what happened! As time went on, control over the state became an end in itself. All that mattered was political power. It got so bad that by Luther's time one of the popes (Julius II) was called the Warrior Pope because he was in battle gear more often than in priestly robes.

What happened to doctrine?

While the church was engaged in this heated struggle for power over the state, doctrinal purity disappeared. The cult of saint worship flourished. The notion that the single life for the clergy was more God-pleasing than the married life became church doctrine. In Germany the married priests were forced to send away their wives, and their children were declared illegitimate.

The idea that Christ was more of a judge than a savior took hold. As a result, people looked to the saints and especially to the virgin Mary for help in time of need. People were taught to trust in their own works, in the works of the saints, and in their church membership for their salvation.

Again, the church survived, but just barely. There were still faithful pastors and teachers. There were still dedicated laypeople. There were still heroes of faith and great church fathers. But their numbers diminished steadily. Although the doctrinal decline cannot be traced exclusively to church-state struggles, those struggles certainly played a role.

In the east the church, the bride of Christ, had become the handmaiden of the state. In the west the bride of Christ wore a sword and fought to be master over the government. In both east and west, the church suffered. Doctrinal purity suffered. Souls suffered; yes, souls were lost.

The Crusades

In 1096 the first crusade began. Seven would follow, including the terrible "Children's Crusade." The Crusades are one of the most fascinating and important movements in history. The motives behind them are many and complicated. The consequences of the Crusades are likewise many and complicated. In the discussion of the roles God has given to church and state, the Crusades mark the height of confusion.

Pope Urban II called on the people of Europe to go to the Holy Land and rescue the sacred places of Christ's life and death from the Muslim Turks. The response exceeded all expectations. From all over Europe people from every walk of life poured into Italy; they were looking for passage to the Holy Land to fight a holy war. Even children came. The ill-fated Children's Crusade ended predictably in disaster; the children died or were sold into slavery.

The question for us here is this: Where did Christ ever ask his church to conduct a war? When did he ever tell us that it was a good work to kill people in order to have the places where he walked in Christian hands? Could anything be further away from the Great Commission to preach and teach the gospel than a holy war?

Even worse than the total confusion of the roles God had given to the church and the state were the other doctrinal consequences of the Crusades. The pope had promised that whoever went on a crusade would not have to go to purgatory when he died; he would go straight to heaven.

But what is purgatory? The Bible says nothing about it. The ancient church fathers never mention it either. Purgatory was a fiction of human imagination. The idea behind it was this: When people die, they really are not yet pure enough to go to heaven, so they go to a place between heaven and hell to be purged of remaining sin and guilt; after purgatory, they can go to heaven.

The notion fit in nicely with the persistent shift of emphasis away from Christ the Savior to Christ the judge, away from God's grace to human works, away from God's Word to human reason.

The Crusades pushed the false doctrine of purgatory to the very center of attention. The idea of purgatory fit perfectly the needs of the pope during the Crusades. The promise of no purging after death was a powerful incentive for the sensitive and guilty to go off to fight this holy war. But the teaching about purgatory did not stop there.

There was no way to pay for the ships and supplies that would be needed to conduct the Crusades, so an additional "indulgence" was proclaimed by the pope: Those who supported and helped pay for the Crusades also would escape purgatory.

So preoccupied had the church become with matters Christ never entrusted to the church that the only real mission of the church was buried. Preoccupation with politics and the earthly kingdom was followed by preoccupation with a murderous war.

Purgatory soon became a central doctrine of the church! It proved an excellent means of raising money. Long after the Crusades were over, the sale of indulgences to get out of purgatory continued and even increased.

Christ the Savior, who died for us and won our salvation, became merely the one who made salvation *possible*. It was up to the church, to the saints, and to the individual Christian to finish the job! When people failed to finish the work of salvation in this life, they could finish it in purgatory after death. And even there the church would aid with indulgences bought and sold as a means of escaping the purging of purgatory.

The church stands or falls on the doctrine of justification through faith in Christ alone. With the promotion of purgatory and indulgences, the church fell! It is not too much to say that the fall was due in large measure to confusing the roles of church and state.

Since Christ had promised that the gates of hell would never prevail against the church, it was now necessary for Christ to act. And act he did. In his rule over history, the Reformation was his divine intervention.

11

Luther and the Early Lutherans

There is no such thing as a lonely false doctrine. False doctrine, like sin itself, always wants company. And also like sin itself, false doctrine always finds company.

Mixing the roles of church and state from the time of Constantine was the result of false doctrine. That false doctrine grew in the company of a shift away from the gospel. Finally it reached its horrible extreme in the Crusades.

The Crusades, to be sure, brought Europe many benefits. The Crusades had important results even for the study of the Bible, with the discovery of many ancient manuscripts. The good, however, that came out of the Crusades only demonstrates a biblical truism: Even out of terrible

evils, God can bring benefits. But at what a cost! Thousands died in war. Even children were sacrificed to a war
sponsored by the church for a goal that had nothing to do
with her assignment to preach the gospel. The worst fatal-
ity of all was the doctrine of justification by grace alone
through faith. The Crusades buried justification under the
rubble of purgatory and indulgences.

Christ had promised that even hell itself could not
destroy the church. With the doctrine of justification
buried, that was exactly the peril that threatened. For
where the heart of the gospel no longer beats, the church
is mortally wounded. Since Christ is true to his Word,
something *had to* happen in history to undo the terrible
loss of the doctrine of justification. Christ had to inter-
vene as the King of history to rescue his church.

The Reformation was the fulfillment in that time of
Christ's promise never to forsake the church. In the work of
Luther and his faithful coworkers, the doctrine of justifica-
tion again was brought to the center of church teaching.

The restoration of the doctrine of justification brought
about a reexamination of all other doctrines in the light of
the Word of God, including the proper roles of church and
state. Therefore it is worth our time to examine at least
briefly the Reformation and the restoration of pure doctrine during the Reformation.

Luther jumped backwards

So many false doctrines had overtaken the church. How
should one begin a reformation?

For Luther the answer became increasingly clear: One
must begin with the Bible and the Bible alone! He
jumped backwards. He jumped over church councils and
popes. He jumped over church fathers and great theolo-

gians. He jumped past tradition and human reason. He jumped straight back to the apostles and the prophets, to Christ himself.

He examined all over again what had been long neglected. The assumption had been this: the church knows; the church is right. Luther started with a very different assumption: God knows; God is right; God has spoken in his Word. A favorite phrase Luther used scores of times in his writings was, "He would not lie to us" or "This is what God's Word says; it will not deceive us."

The Ninety-five Theses

The traditional starting date for the Reformation is October 31, 1517. On that date Martin Luther, the monk, priest, and university professor, nailed his famous Ninety-five Theses to the church door in Wittenberg. Central to the theses was a protest against indulgences and, by implication, against the whole notion of purgatory, which had become so important since the Crusades.

The heart and core of the gospel was at stake in that protest. For if we must rely on our own works either in this world or in purgatory for salvation, then we are lost. We will become either self-righteous Pharisees because of our works, or we will despair because we know our works can never be good enough to cancel out our sin. In either case hell will be our future. For self-righteousness and despair are the opposites of saving faith, of trust in the promise of the gospel.

As Luther and his coworkers went back to the Bible, they rediscovered the buried doctrine of justification. They also discovered many other buried doctrines. Not the least of these was a rediscovery of the roles God had assigned to the church and the state. It was soon clear that a confusion of those roles had played a large part in the destruction of sound doctrine since the time of Constantine.

The difficulty in separating church and state

Recognizing the damage that had been done by the mixing of church and state did not automatically solve the problem. After all, such mixing and confusion had gone on for more than a thousand years. To undo all that would take great wisdom and some time.

We must appreciate the difficulty Luther and his coworkers faced. The dukes and princes owned many of the parish churches. The income from those churches went to the ruler. The university was often owned by the ruler. The University of Wittenberg, for example, where Luther taught, was owned by his prince. A major function of the university was the training of pastors. But the training of pastors should be the responsibility of the church alone.

The union of church and state also presented Luther and those devoted to the Reformation with a very grave political and military problem. The emperor, Charles V, was a staunch supporter of Catholicism. He considered it his duty to support the unity of the church in Germany under the pope. More than once the emperor declared Luther was a heretic and *therefore* an outlaw. Additionally, the emperor considered all who supported Luther to be outlaws.

In collusion with the pope, the emperor tried more than once to put together a military alliance. The goal of the alliance was to swoop down on the "Lutheran" territories in Germany and destroy both Luther and all who supported the Reformation. Though the German constitution made such an action illegal, that did not stop the emperor in his efforts. How could the Lutheran princes defend themselves without revolting?

There were other equally thorny problems: How could the bishops who were also princes continue to hold both positions if they became Lutheran? (Some did.) What would happen to the territories where the ruler was Catholic and the population Lutheran? What about the territories where the reverse was the case? Did a Lutheran prince have a duty to suppress the Catholic religion, since he knew the Catholic Church taught false doctrine? Should he persecute Catholics in the interest of saving their souls?

We only can summarize here how these problems were addressed during the Reformation. There was one guiding principle in all the efforts to answer these difficult questions: God gave the church the gospel; God gave the state the sword; the two should be kept as separate as possible!

The Augsburg Confession

In 1530 those princes who had accepted the Bible-based teachings of Luther made a confession of their faith before the emperor and the German parliament. The emperor himself had requested such a confession from them. That confession came to be a sort of constitution for the Lutheran churches; the date of its presentation to the emperor (June 25, 1530) has been called the birthday of Lutheranism.

It is important to notice that the confession was made in a political forum: before the emperor and the German parliament. It is important to notice that the confession was made by laymen, by princes and civic leaders of German cities. Given the forum and given the ones making the confession, one is surprised at how clear and firm it is on the matter of church and state relations. This is what they said:

Inasmuch as the power of the church or of bishops bestows eternal gifts and is used and exercised only through the office of preaching, it does not interfere at all with government or temporal authority. Temporal authority is concerned with matters altogether different from the Gospel. Temporal power does not protect the soul, but with the sword and physical penalties it protects body and goods from the power of others.

Therefore, the two authorities, the spiritual and the temporal, are not to be mingled or confused, for the spiritual power has its commission to preach the Gospel and administer the sacraments. Hence it should not invade the function of the other, should not set up and depose kings, should not annul temporal laws or undermine obedience to government, should not make or prescribe to the temporal power laws concerning worldly matters. . . .

Thus our teachers distinguish the two authorities and the functions of the two powers, directing that both be held in honor as the highest gifts of God on earth.[4]

Luther and those who were loyal to the gospel with him made every effort to separate church and state at every level.

In military matters and national politics

Since faith is created only by the preaching of the gospel, Luther urged again and again that war in the interest of religion was wrong. The emperor, for example, was planning a new war against the Turks; he wanted soldiers and new taxes to help him with that war. Luther urged: If the war is in the defense of the country, then of course it was the duty of every subject to come to the defense of his homeland. But if the war was a new crusade, a holy war, then it was contrary to the will and Word of God. For God did not give the sword to the state so that it could force people to believe the gospel. Only the Holy Spirit can work faith; and he does that with the Word alone.[5]

If a crusade against the Turks was wrong, what about the emperor's planned crusade against the Lutherans? What should the Lutherans do if the emperor carried out his bloodthirsty plans to attack them as soon as his border with the Turks was secure? The Lutherans banded together in an alliance, but the alliance was purely defensive in nature. The Lutherans refused to revolt against the emperor, even during those times when they were stronger than he was. Any invasion by the emperor would have been completely contrary to German law and to what passed for a constitution. The princes, therefore, felt justified in carrying out the first duty of government: defense of their own people and territory. But revolution, even against an emperor determined to destroy them, was out of the question!

In the Lutheran territories

It is easy to champion a separation of church and state when your own life is threatened by their union. But what happened in the territories where the princes became Lutherans? Did they still champion separation of church and state?

The answer was a decided yes! In most instances the people were ahead of the princes; the people became Lutherans before the prince did. But even so, if the prince was a Lutheran, he did not force those who were not Lutherans to change their religion.

That was in sharp contrast to the behavior of Catholic princes. As far as the Catholic princes were concerned, being a Lutheran was a criminal act. They often violently persecuted Lutherans; they also refused to allow them to worship publicly. But the force used against Lutherans never became an excuse to use force against Catholics in Lutheran territories.

We can see already a pattern of Lutheran behavior developing, a pattern based on the models we have in David, Paul, and the early Christians. The princes resisted the commands of the emperor to return to the Catholic Church—but they refused to rebel. Laypeople in Catholic territories resisted forced "conversion" to Catholicism— but they did not rebel.

The Peasants' War

To be sure, there were instances of religious strife also in the Lutheran territories. Anabaptist sects became popular in much of Germany. Some Anabaptists had illegally seized churches that did not belong to them. Worse still, they incited the peasants to a violent revolt against the state in 1525 (the Peasants' War).

Before the revolt began, the peasants' representatives asked Luther what they should do about their grievances. Luther warned them against violence and revolution, but they ignored his warnings. In fact, they used Luther's teaching about the freedom we have in Christ as their excuse for revolting. When they went on a rampage of looting, burning, and murder, Luther had no choice but to urge the princes to restore order, as was their duty. When the peasants were defeated, Luther pleaded with the princes to show mercy.

Luther has been and still is severely criticized by his opponents for his writings during this sorry period of history. Unfortunately, Luther's opponents then and now prefer to read only the call for action against the rebels. They often fail to consider what Luther wrote before and after the revolt broke out.[6]

Luther took God seriously, and therefore he took all God's Word seriously. He could not ignore what God had said in Romans 13:1-7. Revolution against the state was a sin against God. The state had a right and a duty to restore order. No one had the right to revolt, much less to say that the revolt was in the name of God. That is exactly what the rebel peasants had done.

The prince as Lutheran layman

Many of the princes in Germany became Lutherans out of a sincere conviction that what Luther taught was drawn from the Word of God. They were eager to promote that teaching in their lands. They showed their zeal by urging that parishes be visited to determine the level of Christian education in their territories.

The early visitations of parishes revealed an appalling level of ignorance. People did not know the Apostles' Creed or the Lord's Prayer. The religion of many was nothing but empty form and superstition.

As a result of those visitations, the Lutheran school system was born. Luther wrote his Small Catechism in order to give parents and schools a basic primer in Christian doctrine. It served as the first textbook and reader used in the schools, along with the Bible and a growing number of Lutheran hymns.

The princes were the only ones who had the resources to promote education on the parish level. Likewise they remained the only ones with sufficient wealth to pay for the universities, where pastors and teachers were trained. Often it was the ruler of the territory or the mayor of the town who was responsible for seeing to it that church workers were paid.

The question is, Where should the line be drawn? When does the prince or the mayor cease to be a layman supporting pure doctrine and become a government official controlling the church in the interest of the state?

The consistory

That was a difficult problem for the Reformation. In order to put some distance between church and state, the consistory was established. The consistory was a board of pastors and laymen who administered the affairs of the church. The consistory was usually appointed by the prince. But in the best of cases, once it was appointed, the prince kept his distance from its workings.

In the consistory the lay members, usually lawyers, took care of the temporal and legal concerns of the church. The pastors dealt with the religious concerns, with matters of doctrine and practice.

Some problems were of concern to both the church and the government. For example, marriage and divorce cases were of concern to both. In these matters the consistory sometimes succeeded in keeping the religious and governmental interests separated; sometimes they did not succeed.

The consistory did not perfectly solve the problem of church-and-state separation, but it was a good beginning. Whenever the consistory failed to keep the two apart, there was potential for renewed mischief and for the government to turn the consistory into a department of the state. During the Reformation period, no fixed legal formula was found that would perfectly separate church and state. But the principle remained that the two should strive for separation as much as possible.

Again, we need to remember what a giant leap the Lutherans were attempting to make. They were trying to sort out practices from over one thousand years of history.

In those territories where the prince was Lutheran and most of the population was Lutheran this was the usual way that the prince proceeded:

1. He supported pastors and teachers who taught in accord with the Word of God.

2. When he hired professors at the university, he insisted that they pledge not to teach contrary to the Word of God.

3. If those whose salaries he paid broke their pledge and introduced false doctrine, the prince could arrest them; the arrest was not for false doctrine but for breach of contract.

4. Religious groups that did not teach pure doctrine were not persecuted unless they rebelled; if they preached revolution and acted on that preaching, they were suppressed—again, not because of false doctrine but because of revolution.

5. Inside the empire the Lutheran princes urged the reform of the Catholic Church; when it was clear that Catholicism was not going to be reformed, they refused to revolt against the Catholic emperors. That refusal held in spite of imperial attacks (the Smalcaldic War, part of the Thirty Years' War). They defended themselves and their people but refused to go beyond that.

What about Lutheran princes who were lazy laymen?

When the princes were slow to do their Christian duty, Luther was not slow in rebuking them. His rebukes were directed against princes who did not use their wealth to support education and needy parishes.[7] He warned against laziness in dealing with rebels who would bring war and bloodshed to the people. He scolded two Lutheran princes who were about to go to war with each other over the control of a disputed bishopric that had become Lutheran.

No *Lutheran church-state union*

Luther never urged a union of church and state, however. He never called for the persecution of those who disagreed with him in matters of doctrine. In Wittenberg, for example, there was a religious institution of priests and monks devoted entirely to saying masses for the dead to help get them out of purgatory. They made a good living from it, and they opposed the Reformation. But Luther refused to allow anyone to interfere with them.

Luther and the princes did what they could to separate church and state. In that Luther was way ahead of his times. Few indeed were as eager for such a separation as were the Lutherans. Few worked harder to bring it about.

After Luther's death

Luther's death in 1546 began a period of great turmoil in Germany and in the Lutheran churches. The defensive league of Lutheran princes fell apart. One of the princes, Philip of Hesse, became guilty of bigamy. The emperor, Charles V, wanted to use that as an excuse to attack him and to impose Catholicism on his territory. Another Lutheran prince, Maurice of Saxony, agreed to support the emperor in the war. In exchange Maurice wanted the title and some of the territory of his Lutheran cousin, the Elector of Saxony.

The remaining princes, for the most part, were not interested in fighting to defend a bigamist or in mixing in the affairs of the other two princes.

The result was the brief Smalcaldic War. The emperor was completely victorious. He used his victory and his alliance with the Lutheran Maurice of Saxony to persecute pastors who were faithful to genuine Lutheranism. Thousands of pastors and lay people fled the territories where the emperor and his allies had control.

Ultimately Maurice grew tired of being called a traitor to the Lutheran cause. More importantly, he grew tired of the emperor's failure to keep a number of promises made to him. Maurice attacked and almost captured the emperor. Charles V was finally disgusted with all his troubles in Germany, and he decided to abdicate and retire. His departure made possible the Peace of Augsburg, signed in 1555.

The Peace of Augsburg

According to the peace treaty, Lutheranism was finally recognized in the empire as a legal religion, at least in those territories that had a Lutheran ruler. The succeeding emperors were all Catholics. But they could not make Lutheranism illegal in those territories governed by Lutheran princes.

Princes who were Catholic could continue to persecute Lutherans and did so. Lutheran princes, however, refused to persecute Catholics. The principle held for the Lutherans: It would not be the business of their governments to use the sword in order to create faith! The Lutherans living in Catholic territories either worshiped underground or fled to Lutheran territories for protection and freedom. They did not revolt.

After the Peace of Augsburg, princes devoted to sound doctrine continued as before. They supported churches and schools. When there were doctrinal problems, they supported meetings of pastors and theologians to resolve those problems. It was the princes who encouraged the writing of one of our greatest confessions of faith, the Formula of Concord, in 1577.

Again we note the seriousness with which the Lutheran princes took their responsibilities both as rulers and as Christian laymen. Most of them tried to keep church and state separate. They did not always succeed. There was no recipe or legal formula in Lutheran territories that guaranteed the safety of the church from governmental interference. It was largely up to the individual princes and churchmen to safeguard the separation.

But the goal remained the same as that expressed in the Augsburg Confession, quoted earlier: The church should preach the gospel and not interfere with the civil government; the government should not use the sword to force matters of faith and conscience.

12

Among the Non-Lutherans

Once the Reformation began, it did not stop with the formation of the Lutheran churches. In Luther's day and thereafter, a number of other religious groups emerged. Most of these initially shared Luther's desire to bring about a separation of church and state. Some of them criticized Luther for going too slowly in accomplishing that purpose.

We will consider only one of the major non-Lutheran churches that came out of the Reformation period. We refer here to the Reformed churches. Their spiritual father is John Calvin (1509–1564).

Calvinism

There were and are enormous differences between pure Lutheranism and Calvinism. Those differences are reflected in attitudes towards the state and church-state relations.

Though Luther wanted to separate church and state as much as possible, Calvin falsely accused the Lutherans of turning the church into a tool of the state. Calvin was determined not to make that mistake. He went in exactly the opposite direction: He made the state the servant of the church.

Calvin in Geneva

Calvin did much of his most important work in the city of Geneva. He was determined that the church would not be under the control of the government. But he was even more determined that Geneva should become a city of God on earth.

To that end the church set up rules that governed all aspects of human behavior. When someone violated those rules, that person could be turned over to the civil government for punishment. If someone taught false doctrine, that person too was handed over to the government for punishment.

The most famous example of the church acting with the state against a false teacher is the case of Michael Servetus. Servetus had written against the doctrine of the Trinity. He made the fatal mistake of paying a visit to Geneva. There he was arrested and burned at the stake for heresy (October 27, 1553).

Heresy and politics for Catholics and Calvinists

It is difficult to see much difference between the behavior of the Calvinists and of the Catholics in matters of church-state relations. For both Catholics and Calvinists, heresy was a political, not just a religious, matter. Neither blushed at handing over people found guilty of false doctrine for execution by the state.

Calvin wrote about the different roles God gave church and state in much the same way Luther had written. One, however, sees little evidence of a separation wherever Calvinism became the dominant religion. In German territories where the ruler was a Calvinist, Lutherans and Catholics alike were persecuted by the government.

Why the difference between Calvinists and Lutherans?

How can we account for the striking difference between Lutherans and Calvinists on the matter of church-state relations?

Earlier we noted that the doctrine of justification is the center of the Scriptures. Where that doctrine is clouded or pushed to the side, all other doctrines will be affected and ultimately corrupted. And that is exactly the core of the problem between Calvinists and Lutherans. Calvinists do not see the doctrine of justification as central. In point of fact, the Calvinists deny that Christ died for the sins of the whole world. They deny that the Holy Spirit works faith solely through the gospel in Word and sacraments. Even though many conservative Calvinists taught that the Bible is God's inspired Word, they also insisted on interpreting the Bible in the light of reason. Calvin admitted that much of what the Bible says must be taken on faith alone, but much of what the Bible teaches he refused to take on faith. Much of what he and his successors taught pushed aside the Word of God in favor of reason.

Thus Calvin saw in the Bible that God alone gives faith. From that he concluded with his human reason that God must not want the salvation of those who do not have faith. For God is all powerful; if he wanted someone to believe, they would believe.

Calvin missed the profound mystery in the doctrine of justification: Those who are saved and believe the gospel have only God to thank for it (Ephesians 2:8,9); those who perish in unbelief have only themselves to blame for it (Matthew 23:37). Human reason cannot solve that mystery. Nor does God ask that we solve it. Luther liked to say that when he came upon such mysteries, he simply doffed his doctor of theology cap and figured that the Holy Spirit (the ultimate author of the Scriptures) was smarter than Dr. Luther! Sadly that was not the attitude of the Calvinists.

For Calvin and his followers, the words "God so loved *the world*" of John 3:16 are not literally true. For them none of the many passages that speak of Christ's death for the sins of the world and of God's desire for the world's salvation are to be taken at face value. (Chief among such passages are John 1:29; 3:16; 2 Corinthians 5:19-21; 1 John 2:1,2.)

So the Calvinists denied that Christ died for all and that God earnestly desires the salvation of all through faith in the gospel message. That presented the individual Calvinist with a big problem: If God does not desire the salvation of all, how can I be sure that he desires *my* salvation and that Christ died for *me*? In trying to solve that problem and answer that question, the Calvinists' chief concern switched from proclaiming the gospel and trusting it. Instead, they turned their attention to finding a way to prove by their lives that they were among those chosen for salvation, not those chosen for damnation!

They would set up a "Christian Commonwealth" in which the elect lived and prospered. Their goal would be to prove that they were the chosen of God by advancing the glory of God. They would advance his glory by the kind of lives they led and by the kind of society they established.

That is exactly how the denial of the doctrine of justification ends up in a confusion of the roles of church and state! If we are going to set up a Christian society, then we will need *laws* for that society. Those laws will be taught by the church. But someone will have to enforce those laws given by the church. Enforcing laws is the task of the state, not the church. A society based on laws given by the church needs an enforcer who has the sword; the sword belongs to the state; church and state become mixed!

Thus the church would teach doctrine. It would tell people what to believe and how to live. If people insulted God by believing or living otherwise, then in a truly *Christian* society, they should be punished. Both false doctrine and unchristian living would be crimes against the government.

By their lives and the discipline in their Christian state and society, they would prove that they were among those God wanted to save, not among those God wanted to damn! After all, they were living in a *Christian* society and land. What more proof could one want than that?

Searching for certainty of salvation apart from the gospel is a denial of the doctrine of justification. If we search for it in the kind of society we construct, a society that tolerates only Christian doctrine and Christian life, the mixing of church and state is the result. It becomes the duty of government to enforce what is taught by the church.

But that is not the role God gave to government. In fact, the sword of the government can only create hypocrites; hypocrites outwardly accept by force what their hearts reject. The Holy Spirit uses the gospel in Word and sacraments to create and preserve faith, sound doctrine, and the church. He does not need the sword of the state to do what only the gospel can do.

Theology of the cross or theology of glory?

Calvin and, even more, those who followed him shared with the Catholics a *theology of glory*. They wanted to bring heaven down to earth. They wanted nations and societies that could be called truly Christian. In the pursuit of Christian societies, both Calvinists and Catholics put most of the emphasis on the law, not the gospel. Since they sought a Christian nation and society, it did not seem strange to either Catholics or Calvinists to use the state to assist them in accomplishing their goals.

Luther, on the other hand, was convinced from the Bible that only the Holy Spirit could convert and save. He was convinced on the basis of the Word of God that the only tool the Holy Spirit needed or wanted was the Word itself.

Luther also assumed that the church created by the gospel would remain the suffering church. He took that as a given from Christ's promise of persecution (Matthew 10:17-25) and from the parable of the wheat and the weeds (Matthew 13:24-30). Perhaps most of all, he assumed that the church on earth would always be a suffering church from the simple fact of Christ's suffering. The church imitates Christ in his humiliation. She waits patiently for glory in heaven. Therefore the sword of the state does not belong in the hands of the church.

The whole idea of a city of God on earth was to the Lutherans a contradiction of all that the Bible says about our life on earth. Lutheran theology is rightly called the *theology of the cross*; for now the church carries the cross after Christ. In heaven she will wear the crown.

Catholic and Calvinist swords clash

The mixing of church and state is never harmless. In their pursuit of their own versions of a Christian society, Catholics and Calvinists used the sword of the state to the considerable sorrow of countless thousands. The Thirty Years' War in Germany (1618–1648) started out as a battle between Catholics and Calvinists over control of the state. The Lutherans got caught in the crossfire. By the time the war was over, Germany lay in ruins; two-thirds of its people had perished or become refugees.

In France Calvinist Huguenots battled Catholic kings for control of the state. The Calvinists decided that since the king was a heretic, revolt was legitimate. They came to that conclusion in spite of the fact that Calvin had spoken and written against revolution.

In England and Scotland as well, Catholics and Calvinists battled for control of the state. The Catholic Jesuits plotted the murder of the Protestant Queen Elizabeth. Philip II, the Catholic king of Spain dreamed of a crusade in which he would wipe out the Protestants both in England and in the Netherlands. The Puritan Calvinists revolted against the semi-Catholic King Charles I in England, and in 1649 they beheaded him.

It is sad and sorry history indeed. To be sure, for many who fought in these wars, religion was not the reason but the excuse. Often there were class and economic motives hiding behind a religious mask. Nevertheless, without religion at least some of the wars might not have been fought.

The religion of both Calvinists and Catholics abandoned the Word of God to fight for control of the state. They both had visions of helping God rule history by killing one another and as many Lutherans as got in the way.

The Formula of Concord

In the last great confession of faith of the genuine
Lutherans in Germany, the distinction between proper
concerns of church and government was again clearly
stated. The Formula of Concord in Article XII gives a list
of errors that cannot be tolerated. But the Formula of
Concord separates the list into two parts: errors that cannot be tolerated in the church and errors that cannot be
tolerated in the state.

The Formula of Concord never calls for the state to suppress the errors in doctrine, which the church must suppress by the pure teaching of the Word of God alone. And
it never calls on the church to institute a government that
carries out the will of the church. The church has her work
with souls; the government has its work with outward
behavior in society. The church has her tool, the gospel;
the state has its tool, the sword. The church has her aim,
eternal life; the state has its aim, external order.

When one sees the difference in the work, tools, and
aims of church and state, it is easy to see that the state with
its sword has no role to play in the work of the church. For
justification, grace, and faith are found in the gospel alone.

Both Catholics and Calvinists, on the other hand,
denied the central doctrine of justification. Both operated
with law more than with gospel. Both were more concerned with the fruit on the tree of faith than with the tree;
they neglected faith's creation and care through the gospel
alone. It was easy for them with their law emphasis to see
the state as an ally, for law is the normal and natural business of the state. Both Catholic and Calvinist leaders saw
themselves as God's representatives sent to root out evil
and establish his kingdom on earth. Opposition would be
met with the sword of the state.

13

From the Reformation to the Present

By the end of the period of religious wars in the 1600s, many were disgusted not just with war but also with religion. Rulers and intellectuals began to turn away from religion. That change took place gradually, but it infected all of Europe by the end of the 18th century.

Those who blamed the church for the wars thought that by moving away from the church, peace could be established in the world. They looked for new explanations for life, for history, for humanity's goal and destiny. They looked for such explanations not in the Bible, but in human reason and in scientific investigation.

Saint Augustine, one of the greatest of the early church fathers, prayed, "Lord, you have made us for yourself; our souls are restless until they find their rest in you!" But the Europe of the late 18th century rejected the truth of Saint Augustine's beautiful prayer. Europe turned its back on God.

That turn, of course, also had its effects on church and state relations. We want to consider a few of the most important ideas that came out of the late 18th and early 19th centuries. We still live with the results of the ideas about church and state that came out of the Reformation. But those ideas and their application took on new forms as a result of the thinking and history of the late 18th and early 19th centuries.

New political thinking

Since the time of Constantine, everyone had assumed God was the creator and ruler of the universe. Everyone assumed God had established government and stood behind it. But during the late 18th century, that assumption was challenged. A new assumption arose and took its place. Philosophers were asking questions about the nature of the state. Most of them set the Bible aside completely. They came up with various notions about government, most of which can be summed up with the term *social contract*.

The social contract

According to social contract theories of government, it was not God who established government but humans. People decided for a variety of reasons that they needed government, and therefore they created it.

Jean-Jacques Rousseau (1712–1778) said that since government is the creation of people, people have the right to revolt against it whenever it no longer does what it should.

John Locke (1632–1704) said that government is established by the people but has a tendency to become tyrannical. Therefore a government should have checks and balances in it to keep any one part of the state from becoming dictatorial. Much of Locke's theory about checks and balance was written into the Constitution of the United States.

Adam Smith (1723–1790) challenged the notion that the nation's wealth comes from land and that landowners, therefore, are the natural ruling class. He said that the wealth of the nations comes from labor. Those who create jobs, therefore, are the natural leaders of the nation. His ideas gave respectability to the middle class in its coming revolts against the land-based nobility.

Montesquieu (1689–1755) wrote extensively about the evolution of government. Voltaire (1694–1788) described various theories of contract relationships between the rulers and the ruled.

Again, all these thinkers had this in common: Their theories were based on reason alone.

The American Revolution

The American Revolution of 1776 proved that ideas can be powerful engines of change in history and in society. The rebels were inspired by each of the authors mentioned above. They accepted the social contract theories and assumed that people had a right to revolt, regardless of what the Bible said.

To be sure, when we read the documents that came out of the American Revolutionary War, there are many references to God. But those references often lack any support in the Bible. The authors assumed that what their reason had concluded was as valid as what the Bible says. And what the Bible says had validity only if it agreed with their reason. The American Revolution cannot be justified on the basis of the Word of God, no matter how many times God's name is dragged into it.

During the American Revolution, Lutherans who refused to join in the revolt because of the Word of God were harassed and persecuted. Some Lutherans abandoned what the Augsburg Confession says about government in order to join in the revolt. The man who is often called the father of American Lutheranism, Pastor Henry Melchior Muhlenberg, lamented the action of two of his own sons, who had given up their work as Lutheran pastors to serve the cause of the revolution.

The French Revolution

The American Revolution electrified Europe. Especially in France people were anxious to see if the social contract theories could work in practice. The American Revolution was for them the test. Could people really govern themselves without a king? If so, then perhaps revolution was the wave of the future, as people rose to assert their "God-given rights."

While Europe was still waiting for the final verdict on the ability of the new American government to survive, France exploded in the French Revolution of 1789. The American Revolution had claimed God for itself in the Declaration of Independence. The French Revolution, however, began without any reference to God at all. In fact, it quickly turned anti-religious. In one phase of the revolution, a whole new religion of reason was proclaimed. Churches were closed. Christianity was persecuted.

The writings of the philosophers and the actions of the revolutionaries signaled a new, but not necessarily a better, day for church-state relations.

Napoleon

It is impossible to overestimate the importance of Napoleon Bonaparte (1769–1821). He rose from the ranks of the Corsican middle class to become emperor of France and master over most of Europe.

Napoleon changed everything he touched. And he touched church-state relations. He was not interested in the official atheism of the French Revolution. At the same time, he was without any fixed moral or religious conviction. Of one thing he was certain: He did not want Christians to become a new class of martyrs who might provide the impetus for a revolution against him. Therefore he was not interested in persecuting the church. But Napoleon inaugurated a fundamental change in church-state relations:

1. In France and then in most of the rest of Europe, Napoleon was a champion of freedom of religion.

2. Everywhere Napoleon planted his flag and his boots he seized the property of the church and turned it over to the government.

3. In exchange for the loss of the property, with which the church could support itself at least partially, the church received support from the state; clergy salaries were paid by the government.

By these means Napoleon created what we today call the state-church system in Europe. Freedom of religion for Napoleon was freedom of conscience to believe whatever one wanted to believe or to believe nothing at all. But the church as an organization was not to be free; it was to be tied to the state and dependent on the state.

Recall what we said earlier about German church-state relations. In the Lutheran territories, there really was no fixed legal formula that governed the relationship. With Napoleon's conquests in Germany, that changed. The clergy in Germany, as well as in most of the rest of Europe, became virtual employees of the state. The church could control its own doctrine and discipline its pastors, but otherwise it depended on the state for the salaries of the pastors and teachers.

In the school systems of Europe too, the church lost its influence. Especially in Germany the schools had been parish schools, even when they were paid for by the prince. But after Napoleon's conquests, that all began to change. The state wanted to control education. Schools were to teach patriotism and nationalism; the church could not be trusted with that vital assignment. Even though religion might be taught in the school, it was taught on a state-approved basis.

In reality, loyalty to the state was to take the place of loyalty to a church or loyalty to a set of doctrines taught by a church. With Napoleon nationalism became the new heartbeat of Europe, and that at the expense of loyalty to the church.

Thus there was an outward appearance of greater freedom of religion because Napoleon did not care what church people belonged to. But in reality, the church was very much reduced; it became a servant of the state. In much of Europe, the church was expected to join in the new passion of nations, in the preaching of nationalism: My country, right or wrong, is best. If you visit the great churches of England, you will find the home of one regiment or another. There you will see more symbols of British nationalism and imperialism than you will of Christian faith and doctrine.

After Napoleon

The church-state marriage established by Napoleon has continued to this day and is the norm in Europe. Rulers and governments after the time of Napoleon were, for the most part, as cynical about religion as he was, sometimes even more so.

Governments saw the church as a useful way of keeping the population submissive to the state. Since the government controlled the purse strings, it expected the church to bless whatever the state did. To be sure, the church should always pray for the state and do all she can to prevent revolution and public uproar. But it is not the business of the church to be the government's press or publicity agent.

This forced alliance between the altar and the throne served to separate the faithful from the church. If the government was oppressive, the church was its ally. If the government was hated, how could one be expected to love the church, which blessed all that the government did?

Throughout the 19th century, European governments took over more and more responsibility for the *total* life of the nation. Education, as already noted, moved from a church responsibility to a state responsibility. The government's ownership of the school system changed the emphasis in school from one of primary loyalty to God to primary loyalty to the state.

Health care ceased to be a concern of the church; the government took it over. Caring for the poor and orphans moved also from the church to the state. No longer were givers moved by love to God to support the poor of their parish. They were forced to support the poor of the nation through their taxes. The recipients lost any con-nection to givers motivated by Christian love; the state was the benefactor.

The argument is sometimes made that the state had to take over the responsibilities of education, health, and welfare because the church could not do those things any-more. But why couldn't the church do them? Because she was made a creature of the state! She lost the support, including financial support, of the laypeople. They con-tributed to the church chiefly through taxes forced from them. Why should they pay again on Sunday? With the loss of direct financial support, the church could not carry the increasing expense of education, health, and welfare.

We are not denying that much done by the state was beneficial for many poor and needy people. Nor are we contending that the church would have been able to carry the increasingly heavy load by herself during the age of industrialization. The point is merely this: The church was made so dependent that any role in education or health or charity was largely taken over by the state.

With the state involved in every aspect of human life, the citizen can unconsciously come to see it as god. With-out even thinking about it, the typical mind-set becomes not "The Lord is my shepherd, I shall not want" but "The state is my shepherd, I shall not want."

Given state control of the church and education, health, and welfare, what becomes of the individual Chris-tian's responsibility to serve? How does the Christian show concern for purity of doctrine? The state controls the pas-tors. How does the Christian practice charity? It is all done by the state. Impersonal taxes replace private sacri-

fice for the gospel and for the education of children and
for the care of the poor and needy. In short, the church
becomes irrelevant. Sadly, the individual becomes irrelevant too.

The Prussian Union

When it came to doctrine, the government was interested in harmony between churches. The church is only
good glue for society and support for nationalism if doctrine is not taken seriously. When doctrine is taken seriously, yes, when God is taken seriously, it is necessary to
contend for pure doctrine and to condemn and shun false
doctrine (Matthew 7:15; Romans 16:17,18; Jude 3).

The government wanted harmony in the devotion of
the public to the state. The government was paying the
salaries of the clergy. Pastors and theologians arguing
about doctrine got in the way of the government's ultimate purpose for the church: national unity in support of
the government.

For the Lutherans in Germany, state interest showed
itself chiefly in the Prussian Union. The king of Prussia,
Friedrich William III, decreed the merger of Lutheran and
Reformed churches in his territories into one United
Evangelical Church. The idea spread to other parts of
Germany and took hold wherever there were Reformed
and Lutheran churches existing in the same territory.

Protests about doctrinal difference were of no avail.
The state had decreed it, and that was the end of it.
Lutherans tried to protest within the forced merger. Our
common Lutheran practice of kneeling at Holy Communion comes in part from that protest against the Prussian
Union. Lutherans would kneel when they went to receive
the Sacrament; that was their confession of faith in the

doctrine of the real presence of Christ's body and blood in the Sacrament. The Reformed would stand; that was their way of showing they denied Christ's real presence in the Sacrament.

Soon pastors who still taught the Word of God were persecuted by the officials of the state church. Those officials, employees of the state, were responsible for seeing to it that religion was not a divisive factor in the land. Pastors who did not fit the new mold were arrested, fined, and sometimes put in prison. The only real option for many of them and for their members was flight. In protest against the Prussian Union and the liberalism of the new state churches of Germany, many pastors and faithful Lutheran members came to the United States during the 19th century.

The state-church system remains much as Napoleon created it. The state churches are the official religions of the land. One is born into them and has membership in them by virtue of citizenship. A church tax is levied by the state and is used to pay for pastors and some church buildings.

There really is no struggle anymore in Europe between church and state. But the peace between them is the peace of the graveyard; biblical Christianity is for the most part dead in the state-church system. The primary concerns of the church are with world peace and harmony with nature.

There are exceptions to this norm; but they are few. Some brave Lutherans in Europe have left the state church to form what are known as free churches. They do not receive government support and do not want it. They control their own doctrine and practice, support their own clergy, and train their own pastors. Their lot is an exceedingly difficult one. The free churches are looked upon in society with suspicion. With few exceptions the pastors

and members of some of the free churches are all that is
left of genuine Lutheranism in Europe.

Hegel

We cannot leave Europe until we explore a bit further
this question: If the church is diminished to the role of
handmaid to the state, where do people turn for explanations of the meaning of life and history? If they no longer
trust the church, then where do they look for answers?

The prevailing philosophy is that they should look to
the state itself! The state not only can control the church;
the state can take the place of the church.

The German philosopher Georg Wilhelm Friedrich
Hegel (1770–1831) is a most important teacher of this terrible notion. He gave a certain intellectual respectability
to the growth of the state as it took over functions for-
merly carried out by the church.

Hegel taught that God is constantly evolving and that
his last and most important evolution is in the state itself.
God is in the state; God infuses it with life and energy.
When forms in government change, they are but evidence
for the continuing evolution of God.

So important in Hegel's mind was the connection
between God and the state that Hegel called government
"the saving state"! For if the state and God are all but
identical, then where else but to the state should society
look for salvation?

It is impossible to overemphasize the importance of
Hegel's thought on the modern world. Listen to almost
any campaign slogan in Europe or in the English-speaking
world. Behind the slogans you will see a smiling Hegel!
Whatever is wrong in society, the state should be able to
fix it.

When people accept what Hegel taught, what happens to church-state relations? Again we note that in those countries with a state-church system, the church becomes increasingly irrelevant. All the major problems of life become political problems, and solutions are sought in parliament, political parties, and campaigns for political office.

What about those countries that do not have a state-church system? What about those countries where the churches are still alive and free and healthy? There the temptation is great and growing for churches to meddle even more in politics than ever before. For the assumption remains that the state has the solution *and* the power to enforce the solution. If the church wants a voice and role, then it can find that voice and role only through political action. Does that sound familiar? Perhaps 99.9 percent of American citizens have never heard of Hegel. But his ideas are alive and well and flourishing as much in the United States as anywhere else.

Karl Marx

The most extreme form of "the saving state" idea comes to us from Karl Marx (1818–1883), one of the founding fathers of modern communism. He took the ideas of Hegel and went several steps farther.

Marx took God out of Hegel's philosophy. In fact, in the *Communist Manifesto* of 1848, Marx considered religion the opium that drugs the masses into mindless submission. Given what we have already noted about the cynical alliance between the throne and altar in Europe, Marx was not altogether wrong. Where the state uses the church for its own ends, there the church serves little purpose beyond that described by Marx. It keeps people quiet with the promise of a better life in heaven.

Since Marx was an atheist, he came to his interpretations of history altogether apart from the Word of God. His ideas about man and man's destiny were completely contrary to the Word of God. The goal of history, according to Marx, was the triumph of the working class. History would reach its goal when violent revolution overthrew all government in favor of the dictatorship of the working class.

The working class would set up a temporary government to get rid of rulers and employers and the church that blessed them. Such a government would destroy all inequality and usher in the Marxist goal of history, a veritable heaven on earth. Once government under the dictatorship of the working class had done its work, then government could fade away. All the workers of the world would live in a workers' paradise on earth.

As far as Marxists were concerned, religion, especially Christianity, only gets in the way of that ultimate triumph of the working class. Christians submit; to Marxists that was bad. Christians help the poor and the suffering; to Marxists that was even worse. For only when suffering was made greater would people be miserable enough to risk the revolution Marx called for.

Marx taught that once the great revolution took place, people would work together in harmony for the common good. An important communist principle was, From each according to his ability; to each according to his need.

Marx expected that those who could contribute much to society by their labor would gladly take no more from their work than they needed. That assumes people are not greedy. It assumes people are good. It assumes there is no original sin inherited from Adam and Eve.

But there is original sin. And because of it Marxism simply cannot work. Most people will conclude: If I can get my salary, health care, education, and housing with minimal or no effort, why should I work hard? Just so someone else can have the same thing? No, I will work hard if I get something by way of a reward for it, otherwise not.

Most governments set up on the basis of Marxist principles have collapsed. They collapsed in no small part because of the denial of original sin. People simply do not automatically work together for the common good. Even consistent and severe levels of force cannot get most people to abandon "me first!" thinking.

The church, of course, played no role in Marxist states. Communist governments were all officially atheistic governments. But it is interesting to note yet once more that Christians did not revolt even against Marxist governments.

It is equally interesting to note that the turn away from Christianity had as its excuse the wars of religion. How much better off has the 20th century been with a state-church system and with states that promoted atheism? Has there been less bloodshed, less human suffering inflicted by fellow humans? Has the soul found peace?

Capitalist democracies

In those countries where Hegel is an influence but not Marx, capitalist economies within the framework of democratic political institutions have been the rule. Let not those who live in these countries be too quick to call their societies "Christian countries" just because they are not Marxist or communist.

Let us remember that communism failed because it ignored fallen human nature and that capitalism works in large measure because it takes advantage of human greed and makes a virtue out of it. That's not quite what Paul had in mind in 1 Timothy 6:6-10!

We make the point merely in the interest of keeping clear in our minds that the church has no commission from God to bless one form of government or one economic system as though God had instituted that form, that system.

Just as capitalism makes a virtue out of greed, so just below the surface of much democratic philosophy is the same denial of original sin important to communist governments. Almost all the fathers of modern democratic principles assumed people are basically good. They assumed human reason alone could bring the triumph of good and justice without any guidance from the Word of God. They assumed what people decided by a democratic vote was right simply because the majority decided it. They assumed our greatest needs are political needs.

Their descendants have gone beyond them; most citizens assume their greatest needs can either be satisfied by the state or should be guaranteed by the state. How strange must Christ's quotation from the Old Testament sound to them: "Man does not live on bread alone, but on every word that comes from the mouth of God" (Matthew 4:4). How peculiar these words of Jesus must be in their ears: "Seek first [God's] kingdom and his righteousness, and all these things will be given to you as well" (Matthew 6:33). Even if the state could supply or guarantee all physical needs, these words of Jesus are still true: "What good will it be for a man if he gains the whole world, yet forfeits his soul?" (Matthew 16:26).

If we are going to understand church-state relations in the modern world, we need to keep in mind the path those relations have traveled. If we forget the history, we will not see the dangers of mixing church and state. If we forget the Scriptures, we will not see the folly of mixing church and state.

If we are going to be Christians and citizens, we need to avoid both extremes: We need to shun the extreme of separation from society and the state; we need equally to avoid the notion that ours is the truly Christian society and Christian state with all the answers to life's problems, answers given by God—or by us, if we just join and influence the right political party.

Part III

Current Problems in
Church-State Relations

14

The State over against the Church

We have considered what the Bible has to say about the Christian as a temporary citizen of the earthly kingdom. We have seen from history how Christians from biblical times to the present have served the state with honor and with loyalty to the Word of God. We have also seen what damage is done when church and state forget the distinct roles and work God has given to each.

We turn now to a consideration of church-and-state relations in the United States of America. What is and what should be the relationship between the church and the state in the United States?

An absolute separation is impossible

Citizens of the United States can give thanks to God for a government that has tried to keep church and state separate. There is a remarkable degree of religious freedom in the United States compared to civil governments over history and in other places of the world. Churches in the United States have been allowed to develop by and large without governmental control. Some Lutherans have rejoiced that in America the Lutheran teaching of the separation of church and state has had an opportunity to be implemented.

However, even in the United States, the church exists inside the framework of the earthly kingdom. We cannot escape that fact. Since that is so, there can be no real thought of an absolute or a total separation of church and state. The Lutherans in Germany found that out in the 16th and 17th centuries; it is true for us today as well.

The church exists inside the state

The law of the land also applies to churches. The organizations of the church are incorporated under state and federal laws. The constitutions of congregations, school federations, and other church-related organizations are all on file in some state office. The publishing house that prints this book is a legal corporation subject to corporation law in the State of Wisconsin.

The church also can benefit from her existence inside the framework of the state. Our churches enjoy police and fire department services. Most of our church workers pay social security taxes and are eligible for benefits from the Social Security Administration. Students for the preaching and teaching ministry in our schools benefit from government aid programs. Children in our Lutheran elementary schools receive governmental subsidies for some food and health services; transportation and some textbooks may be provided at state expense.

State regulation of the church

To some extent the state also regulates activities of the church. Religious organizations risk their tax exempt status if they become involved in political activity. Schools operated by the church must abide by laws pertaining to health and safety. Some states try to regulate attendance policy, teacher certification, or even curriculum.

Pastors or teachers who violate standard codes for ethical behavior while ministering to troubled members or students cannot hide behind a separation of church and state. They are subject to lawsuits and prosecution. If the church-at-large knew of a pattern or tendency towards abusive or otherwise illegal behavior in a worker, the church body can be sued for not protecting its members.

We could multiply examples. But perhaps these few are sufficient to demonstrate the point that any total separation of church and state is impossible. How to keep that connection from becoming a problem of improper mixing is a challenge for us, just as it was for our forebears.

The United States Constitution

Church and state relations in the United States have as their starting point the First Amendment and the Fourteenth Amendment to the United States Constitution.

The pertinent words of the First Amendment are, "Congress shall make no law respecting an establishment of religion or prohibiting the free exercise thereof." Initially these words applied only to the relationship of the federal government to the church. In 1940 a Supreme

Court decision (*Cantwell v. Connecticut*) removed that lim-
itation. Using the Fourteenth Amendment, the Supreme
Court declared that the First Amendment also applies to
states; states cannot make laws respecting the establishment of religion or prohibiting its free exercise.

The First Amendment contains two famous clauses that
have become battlegrounds in church and state relations.
The two seem to contradict each other when they are
applied. The apparent contradiction has created considerable tension between church bodies and between some
religious groups and the government.

The Establishment Clause

The Establishment Clause of the First Amendment
says, "Congress shall make no law respecting an establishment of religion." It is designed to guarantee a high degree
of separation—some have called it a wall of separation—
between church and state. The government cannot do
anything that would give the appearance of favoring one
church over another. It cannot do anything that would
show a preference for Christianity over a non-Christian
religion. It cannot give the appearance of favoring religion
over atheism.

The Establishment Clause is designed to guarantee that
no one will be compelled by the government to support a
religion through his or her taxes. It assures that there will
be no state church in the European sense of the term in
the United States.

The courts have ruled on the basis of the Establishment
Clause that organized or compulsory prayer and the teaching of the Bible as the Word of God in public schools is
unconstitutional. Likewise, the posting of the Ten Commandments on government buildings or in schools and

nativity scenes on public property have been declared illegal in many places. According to the court interpretation of the Establishment Clause, there is to be no use of government property that might suggest the government approves of or supports religion, any religion.

The problem with the Establishment Clause

The Establishment Clause assures us of a secular government. At first glance that would appear to be ideal. It would seem to be exactly what we want when we call to mind the different work God has given to church and state. But the government in the 20th century is much more involved in the daily lives of citizens than the writers of the Constitution and the author of the First Amendment ever could have imagined possible. The government dominates in the fields of education on every level, in health and welfare concerns, in life-and-death decisions for the unborn and for the old. When government activity so dominates a culture, there is the danger that a secular government can equal a godless society.

In no sphere of activity is the danger of such an equation more threatening than in the education of our children. The Establishment Clause guarantees a secular government, but it also guarantees a secular education for those in government-controlled schools. If a secular education equals a godless education, we have reason for serious concern.

The government as educator?

Those who control the educational system to a large extent control the worldview of the nation. Therefore we want to examine carefully the role of government in education and the impact it has on the work of the church.

Children spend some of the most formative hours of their lives in the government's care if they attend public school. But the Establishment Clause essentially means that a favorable view of God and religion are excluded from the classroom. If God and religion are considered irrelevant in that instruction, families are confronted with a serious problem. How will they counter the false notion that God and his Word play no part in human history? How will they combat the terrible prospect that their children will grow up thinking that life without God is an acceptable option?

It is very difficult to counter all the hours of irreligious and sometimes anti-religious instruction with but two years in confirmation class and a couple hours on Sunday morning!

Our whole view of ourselves, our world, our purpose, and our destiny comes from the Word of God. But that is not the view taught in most school systems. Rather this is the point of view:

- People are basically good.

- Churches are all equal; one religion is just as good as another, and no religion at all is just fine too.

- Talk of sin gives children a poor self-image; therefore speak instead of poor choices.

- Guilt does not need forgiveness; it needs therapy.

- Immorality, vice, and perversion do not need correction; they need an appreciation for alternative lifestyles.

- There is no such thing as absolute truth outside math and some sciences; therefore find truth in yourself and in how you feel.

The problem becomes obvious if we again remember a fundamental principle we have been discussing throughout this book: God gave the sword to the state for the regulation of *outward behavior*. But the process of education always goes deeper than outward behavior. Education involves more than facts. It involves motives. It involves attitudes. It involves the ability to make judgments about truth and falsehood, about good and evil.

When the task of educating the youth is handed over to the state, the state is stuck with a bad set of choices: Does it teach religion? If so, whose religion? Does it avoid religion? Then it must teach a view of life that is inherently irreligious, if not anti-religious.

The challenge to parents

We would not want the Establishment Clause repealed. We favor a secular government. But we must realize that a secular state is also a problem for us. Christian parents must realize that it is up to them to teach their children right from wrong. They must realize that takes time. They must realize that often their teaching of the truths of God's Word will run directly counter to what their children are taught in school.

There is no doubt about it: Christian parents are confronted with a daunting challenge, made all the more daunting in a society where both parents may have to work outside the home and in homes where there is only one parent.

Throw into the mix the dominance of television in the nonschool hours. Television programs will only strengthen the impression in children that there is no absolute right and wrong and that God is not an important factor in the lives of most successful people or happy people.

The Free Exercise Clause

Many have tried to undo what they consider the damage done by the Establishment Clause. They argue in the political arena and in the courts that the Free Exercise Clause is being violated when God is excluded from public life and from schools.

The Free Exercise Clause of the First Amendment says, "Congress shall make no law prohibiting the free exercise thereof [that is, of religion]." When the Bill of Rights was added to the Constitution, no one thought there was a contradiction between the Establishment Clause and the Free Exercise Clause. The first clause was designed to assure separation of church and state; the second clause was designed to prevent persecution of any religion by the state.

But in recent years, many Christians have sought to use the Free Exercise Clause as a way around the "wall of separation" in the Establishment Clause.

The argument goes like this: If the government forbids Bible reading and prayer in the public schools, it is preventing the free exercise of religion. If the government's school system teaches values contrary to those of the families whose children are in the schools, that too violates the Free Exercise Clause. If the government forbids public displays of the religion of citizens, it is interfering with free exercise.

In countless court cases, the two clauses have been pitted against each other. The so-called Christian or Religious Right has placed itself behind an emphasis on the Free Exercise Clause. Opposing the Christian Right, groups like Americans United for the Separation of Church and State have organized to sue for a strict interpretation of the Establishment Clause.

Should we join the Religious Right in court?

We lament with good reason the growing godlessness of our society. But joining with religious groups in court is not the answer to the problem. We must continually return to the principle that God has given his Word to the church and the sword to the state.

It is not the business of the state to teach doctrine. It is not the business of the state to write prayers or organize their recitation. It always harms both church and state when the state gets mixed up in the work of the church.

But someone may ask: How can it hurt if everybody says the Lord's Prayer together in school? What harm would it do if some other prayer were recited, so long as it did not offend anyone's religion? Wouldn't it help to establish some sort of discipline and order in increasingly unruly children if there was some devotional activity at the beginning of the school day?

The harm is this: The true worship of God comes only from faith created by the gospel. Any other worship is idolatry. Do we really want our children saying prayers that are not based on solid biblical truth? Even if the prayer is the Lord's Prayer, do we really want to give the impression that God is satisfied as long as you pray, regardless of what he says in his Word, regardless of faith in that Word, regardless of life based on his Word?

In point of fact, it hurts the mission of the church when people are left with this notion: All I have to do is pray, and God ought to be satisfied with me; that's what I learned in school. If that's the case, why bother with hearing his Word and keeping it? If "all I have to do is pray," what purpose do the Bible, the sacraments, even Christ serve?

We do not want to worship together when there is no unity in the confession of faith and doctrine. Even less do we want to worship in a setting where the Scriptures are set aside altogether. By joining in such worship, we surely give the impression that faith, doctrine, and loyalty to Christ and the Scriptures do not matter. Jesus warned against such worship repeatedly. In fact, there is scarcely a book in the Bible that does not attack careless and faithless worship.

Even if by some miracle all these objections could be resolved, we would still be left with the basic problem that God did not give the care of souls, his Word, sacraments, preaching, or prayer to the state. The state's business is outward behavior, not the care of souls. The Scriptures make that clear. The reading of history shows what disaster follows when the Scriptures are ignored on this subject.

We want to worship together on the basis of the Word purely taught and the sacraments rightly administered. And we want that Word taught by those who are loyal to it. Where are such to be found? In church! That's where the Word and sacraments are and are supposed to be! That is the way that God wants it! That is the way we will do it, even though it means a much higher degree of responsibility for our parents and our congregations.

Where possible, our children may attend our Lutheran schools. Others may be taught at home by their parents or groups of parents. That solves part of the problem. But for most of our families, Lutheran schools and home schooling are not options. Where the public school is the only real possibility, the *church* needs to do everything it can to assist parents in carrying out the Great Commission at home.

It is, however, not the business of the church to look to the state to do what the church or parents are unwilling to do. If we do not share the pure Word with our children, the state cannot do it and should not be asked to do it for us.

Beyond question, our parents and our parishes are confronted with an enormous challenge. Theirs is a most serious responsibility. Getting the job done in a couple hours on Sunday morning plus a couple years in confirmation class hardly seems adequate. The role of the parents is always primary. The energy of the church and the cooperation of parents in the raising of our children has never been more difficult. It has also never been more important.

What about state aid to church schools?

Many are looking for some middle ground between the Establishment Clause and the Free Exercise Clause of the First Amendment. Might there be a way for the government to support private schools without violating the Establishment Clause?

Some of the arguments in favor of finding ways to increase state aid to private schools are the following:

1. Some parents object to schools in which teaching is from an anti-Christian bias as much as other parents object to schools teaching from a Christian bias.

2. Christian parents pay taxes too. Why shouldn't some of their taxes go to the support of a school that promotes their religious convictions? Why must all of it go to support schools that teach contrary to their religious convictions?

3. Requiring children to attend schools that teach contrary to their own religious principles violates the Free Exercise Clause.

4. If state aid were available to any and all schools, regardless of their religious convictions, the Establishment Clause would not be violated.

5. Expanded state aid to nonpublic schools furthers the democratic ideal. Currently only those with enough money for tuition can send their children to nonpublic or Christian schools. If the taxes spent on education were portable, even the poor could afford an education that reflected the convictions of the family.

Having taxes portable for educational purposes means simply this: If the state spends $4,000 per student per year to subsidize local school systems, then all or part of that could be spent by the student in the school of his or her family's choice; the student could carry state aid with him or her.

There is some legal precedent for these arguments. Court cases in the past that addressed the issue of state aid to private and church-related schools have often resolved the tension between the two clauses in the First Amendment this way: Direct aid to church-related schools violates the separation of church and state in the Establishment Clause, but aid that goes to the student does not.

With those court cases as precedent, the state already supports private education indirectly in a number of ways. Some of those ways were mentioned at the beginning of this chapter. Many states provide school bus transportation for students in private schools. Health and counseling services are available at state expense to students in nonpublic schools. Textbooks that are used in the public school can in some states be supplied also to nonpublic schools. All these forms of aid come under the heading of aid to the student, not aid to the school.

The same precedent exists in colleges and universities. In higher education federal and state government programs that aid students with their college expenses are open to students in private and church-related schools.

They are even available to those who plan to study for full-time service in the church. The one major stipulation is that the school attended be accredited by some independent outside agency recognized by the government. That requirement is designed to protect both the government and students from scam schools, schools that crank out diplomas without providing a legitimate education. Again, the aid is viewed as going to the student, not to the school or its religious sponsor.

State aid to church schools is not without its problems

The question is, Does the aid already provided to students rather than directly to the schools improperly mix church and state? Would expanded state aid through something like a voucher system (portable taxes for educational purposes) entangle church and state in one another's work to a dangerous degree?

We need to recognize the dangers present in any kind of aid that benefits church schools. Even the aid that goes to the student and not directly to the school may come with a price tag attached to it. As appealing as the pro-aid arguments may appear, we must ask some serious questions.

For example, will the government give the aid only to students in schools that accept government regulation? Could such regulation include regulation of the curriculum or practices that reflect the doctrinal position of the church? If such regulation is not part of the aid today, what assurances do we have that it will not become part of the aid tomorrow? Governments change. Attitudes dominant in government change. Regulations follow those changes.

Let us say, for example, that the school teaches the biblical doctrine of creation. Let us say that it condemns most abortions and the practice of homosexuality as sins that damn the impenitent. Let us say that the school insists that God has given different roles to men and women and that those roles must be reflected in the positions of authority assigned at the school. Let us say that the school refuses to hire teachers who do not hold to a set doctrinal position. Let us say that the school reserves the right to expel students who reject the religious position of the school.

What happens to the government aid to students attending that school? Can it be cut off because the religious views of the school do not reflect current thinking in the government on these questions?

Already one religious college has run into legal difficulty. The difficulty came not because of the quality of education in the school, which was not questioned, but because of the distinction made on the campus between men and women. Students lost their right to participate in government aid programs because of the application of a doctrinal principle at that school.

For our purposes here, it is not necessary to discuss the right or wrong of that school's doctrinal position. The point is that the government disapproved of a doctrinal position at a school; for that reason its students lost access to government loan and grant programs.

Do our schools run a similar risk? Can government aid to students be cut off because of a doctrinal position taken by the school? Some might answer that we need to keep a watchful eye on that possibility. But until the government improperly interferes with our doctrine and its application, we will accept the aid for our students. If the day comes when the government interferes, we will refuse the aid.

Is life ever really that simple? A school grows because of aid given to students by the government. Buildings are erected. Staff is in place. Suddenly government regulations change. But the school has become dependent on the students who could not be there were it not for government support. Now what will happen?

The real problems have just begun! Will we refuse those students admission now because without government aid they cannot afford our school? Will we dismiss half the faculty and close half the buildings that are not yet paid for because we no longer have the students for those teachers and buildings? Or will we try to find some clever way of satisfying a government regulation at the expense of faithfulness to the Word of God? Will we buy the argument that it's just a small compromise, and given the choices, it is the best choice of a bad lot? Will our people say, A slightly flawed Christian education is better than no Christian education at all! Will our congregations say, We are stuck with the debt on these buildings, and we cannot throw the faculty out on the streets; we have no choice but to compromise!

Government funds come with government regulation. The power of the state to change the regulations is virtually without limit. On the other hand, the appetite for the aid is also without limit. Government aid can become an addictive drug for a nonpublic school system.

Many outside the church oppose such aid. They argue that aid to students ultimately is aid to the schools. They make the case that the school benefits as much as the individual student. Therefore, they maintain, such aid does violate the Establishment Clause.

Still others argue that such aid might not violate the Establishment Clause; but nevertheless, when it is given, the government should have the right to impose social values accepted by the majority of taxpayers as a condition of such aid. Thus if faculty is hired or called based on religion, the state should view that as illegal discrimination on the basis of religion. Likewise, they argue that dismissing students or teachers because of their religious views violates the civil rights of those dismissed. They maintain that if a school does that, it should not benefit from the public purse.

A fundamental objection to any kind of state aid, direct or indirect, is raised by those who share Napoleon's view of the public school system: The schools are there to help unify the country. In their opinion Christian schools emphasize divisions and therefore are a socially negative influence in the country. In their opinion Christian schools undermine nationalism and the sense of united national purpose that schools should foster.

Those who raise this objection actively lobby against any kind of aid. But they do not stop there. They are often active as well in trying to impose burdensome regulations on nonpublic schools. The purpose of the regulations is either to get rid of such schools altogether or at least to make the operation of the schools more difficult. Increasing the difficulties may discourage others from beginning such schools.

The battles between those who favor greater government aid and those who oppose any aid at all appear to be heating up. As state governments move to expand aid to nonpublic schools, the number of court cases will surely increase.

But the pressure to accept such aid will increase as well. Whether the aid is indirect or direct, parents who are unhappy with public education will put pressure on churches and church schools to accept the aid those parents need if their children are to receive a Christian education.

As understandable as the pressure of such parents may be, the church needs to exercise the greatest caution when accepting any kind of support from the state for her schools. No hard and fast rule can be made about the acceptance of aid for students or aid to schools. But those who imagine such aid comes without a price tag may well be in for a rude surprise.

We need to come back again and again to the basic principle that God gave the church the gospel and the government the sword. We do not want the government to tell our schools what to teach or how to discipline for false doctrine. That's not the government's business. But the power of the purse is the power to rule and regulate. If the government gives aid, the government assumes a right to regulate where and how that aid is used.

What about other forms of aid to the church?

It has been standard practice throughout history that church property used for religious purposes is not subject to taxation. It has likewise been the norm in the western world that the income of the church is not subject to corporation taxes. Church workers pay taxes just like everyone else. But churches themselves do not.

Isn't that a form of state aid to the church? Do we refuse such aid or object to it in any way? Does the exemption violate the principle of separation of church and state?

Increasingly, these questions are being asked by those outside the church. Cities especially look with longing on the property of churches exempt from property taxes; they would dearly love to tax such property in order to relieve the growing burden of the property tax on individual home and land owners.

We should say from the start that the state for centuries has granted such exemptions for reasons of its own. The state has recognized that the service provided by churches is of benefit to the nation.

Church members on the whole tend to be more law-abiding than nonchurch members. Churches provide support for their members that the state could provide only at much greater expense. It is assumed by governments that counseling received from clergy saves the state the expense of such services. And even though the government has taken over much of the work of supporting the needy, the church still does that work too on a limited basis. To the extent that it is done by the church, the government saves its own scarce revenues. The church is involved in helping her members in all kinds of situations, which serves the ultimate purpose of the state: maintaining an orderly society.

The state has accordingly been reluctant to discourage the work of the church that is very beneficial to society by taxing churches. So far the traditional forms of tax exemption have been without any conditions, apart from the expectation that the income and property of the church are used for genuinely religious purposes.

Our churches, therefore, have appreciated and made use of the exemptions. At the same time, we recognize that the government could change its mind about the exemptions at any time or decide to impose unacceptable conditions on such exemptions. In the more than 1,500 years of experience, however, that has not been a serious problem.

Local governments are beginning to ask property-tax-exempt organizations to contribute voluntarily to the public purse. The voluntary contribution should help the government cover the cost of some government services enjoyed by exempted institutions. It is argued that the expense for trash pickup and fire and police protection for church property should be paid by those who receive these benefits; that includes churches. We have no right to object on moral grounds to such requests.

If the government decided to tax church incomes and property used for religious purposes, we might object on the grounds of separation of church and state. But the argument by the church would be a weak one. We might argue that government tax laws always are designed to favor activity beneficial to the state; therefore church income and property should continue to enjoy its exemption. But should such arguments be rejected by the state, our churches would have no choice but to pay the taxes. We are subject to the law of the land. The church will not revolt.

Improper cracks in the First Amendment

In some areas of national life, the government traditionally has done work that properly belongs only to the church. Today those areas are under closer examination than ever before as the two clauses of the First Amendment are debated and fought over in court.

The most prominent example of a crack in the First Amendment is the government's practice of hiring chaplains for the armed forces, prisons, and some government-run hospitals.

To be sure, the government does not hire chaplains because it has a desire to promote the gospel. It hires chaplains for the sake of morale and perhaps morals in the institutions mentioned. Nevertheless, we have reason to object to the practice. Again, care of souls is not the work

God has given to the state. The state is to concern itself with outward behavior.

Certainly the souls and the minds of soldiers, prison inmates, and hospital patients are important. But care for them is the work of the church; it is the work the Holy Spirit does through the proclamation of the law and the gospel. It should be a scandal if churches fail to take care of the souls of their members in the armed forces, prisons, and hospitals.

Thus our objection is based on a principle taught by the Word of God. It is based on a principle that history has taught us to guard carefully. The principle is, as so often stated earlier, The state has the sword, the church has the gospel.

But there are other reasons for a principled objection. A chaplain hired by the state is obliged to do the bidding of the state. If a soldier or prisoner or patient wants that chaplain's services, it cannot be on the basis of the pure Word of God alone. That's not why the government hired the chaplain. The services must appeal to the broadest range of people, lest any be offended.

None of the apostles or prophets, certainly not Jesus himself, could have served under such conditions. In the government-run chaplaincy, there really is no room for an uncompromising "This is what the Lord says!"

Therefore it is altogether proper and important that the church should call her own chaplains to carry the gospel to her people where they are. Personal contact from a parish pastor or from a chaplain called by the church is best. When that is not possible, pastors, family, and friends can share letters and tapes. Regardless of the difficulty that the church and families and individuals may have, the business of caring for souls is not the state's business.

Again and again we need to repeat that God did not give the gospel to the state; he gave it to the church.

Of course, insisting on the principle that worship is always to be according to the Word of God is often inconvenient. Of course, refusing the efforts of the state in its chaplaincy services requires greater effort from the church and from families. Of course, it means we have to do a good job of training our members and our children in the truth of God's Word. That, finally, is the only way we will be able to remain faithful in whatever place we may be, which is exactly the assignment that Christ has given to the church and to her people in the Great Commission!

Let those who want the state to carry out the work of the church go back and consider all the harm that has been done in the past by such a false doctrine and practice! It makes no difference that the motive is good. The motive was good in the past too. But it was wrong. It was contrary to the Word of God. It was doomed, therefore, to cause more harm than good.

15

The Church over against the State

In the previous chapter, we considered the problem of the state in the church. But that is only one side of the coin. There is also the problem of the work of the church as it comes into contact with the state.

The "prophetic role" of the church

The church carries out her mission in the world as she brings God's Word to people. The message of the law goes out to both the rulers and the ruled. It rebukes sin and drives us to despair because we have not kept the law and cannot keep it. The ultimate goal of that preaching of the law is to crush all sinful human pride and destroy in us any thought that we could save ourselves, be righteous before God, or even contribute in some small way to our own salvation.

After the law has been properly proclaimed and received, people are ready for the gospel. They are ready to be brought to new life through the message of grace. The gospel is the good news that God, in spite of us, has sent his Son to be our Savior. It is the message that Jesus our Savior has taken away the sins of the world by his perfect sacrifice for us and in our stead. It is the message that our exalted Savior rules over everything in heaven and on earth for the benefit of his church. It is the good news that he will finally bring this age to an end and take all of his church to himself in heaven.

The message of the law and the gospel is the only message the church has. It addresses all members of the society in which the church carries out her mission. That's what we mean by the prophetic role of the church. She carries her message to all. If rulers are corrupt, corruption should be rebuked by the law. If society has decayed, the warning of the law should not be muted or muffled. For on account of such decay, as the Scriptures clearly testify, nations perish under God's righteous judgment.

The prophetic call of the gospel to society is a call to all the people in it: Bend the knee in humble confession and then in faith before the crucified and risen Savior. He alone can rescue and redeem. He alone can save rulers, the nation, and society from the righteous judgment of God against the wickedness of a culture that has turned its back on him and his Word.

Thus if the government passes laws that permit and sanction what God forbids and condemns, the church must speak out. If the church says nothing, her own members will be seduced without a clear warning cry from the prophet's trumpet (Ezekiel 33). Just as terrible, the unbeliever will see and hear no call to repentance if the church never condemns sin in society. And if unbelievers hear no call to repentance, how will they ever hear of the ultimate and only solution for sin, the forgiving grace of Christ?

As the church carries out her prophetic role, she preaches law and gospel. She does it not on Mars or Jupiter. She does it here and now on Earth in the context of the society in which she lives and works. Society and governments condone abortion, promote gambling, sanction premarital sexual unions, and accept the notion that the human race is the product of evolution. The church must tell all what God says about those things.

In the name of freedom of speech, every depravity is for sale on the street corner. Society is driven by greed and the lust for power. The church must proclaim the Word of God against those sins. She is unfaithful to her Lord and her mission if she searches for something else to talk about, lest someone be offended. People *should* be offended if they are guilty. How else will they know the anger of the Lord and be prepared by the Holy Spirit for the saving message of the gospel?

An important limitation

The aim of the prophetic mission of the church is the salvation of souls, not the reformation of society. It is not the business of the church in carrying out her prophetic role to become actively involved in politics. When the Word of God is preached to rulers, it is the same law and gospel that is preached to plumbers and carpenters.

The church does not tell the plumber how to do plumbing. She does not tell the carpenter how to build a house. That's not the mission of the church. She does not tell the ruler how to rule either. That's also not her mission. She proclaims the law and the gospel, nothing more and nothing less.

The church does not help the legislator draft laws. She does not tell the mayor or the governor or the President which bills to sign and which to veto. She does not tell the judge what penalty to inflict for a crime and what mercy to show for an offense. None of those things are the work of the church. They are all the work God has given to the state.

The church also has no business telling the voter how to vote. That is the business of Christians *as citizens*, not the business of the church. We have noted earlier that Christians will carry their Christian convictions with them into the voting booth. But it is the Christian's personal duty to find out the positions of the candidates for office. The church is there to educate Christians from the Word of God for time and for eternity. Christians do not need the church to do their thinking for them in applying the Word of God to specific candidates for public office.

Nor do Christians need the church to tell them exactly what they should do in the political arena about all the evils of society mentioned earlier. All of us have the duty to examine our own lives in the light of the Word of God and to struggle against the fallen world around and within us. All of us have the duty to consider what we can do as citizens to be light and salt in a dark and perishing world. The church as an organization of Christians must not take the place of Christians in action in society. For the church needs to remain church: It proclaims the law and the gospel to the world.

Many think that the church should make it easier for them. The church should campaign for a political party and actively pursue the defeat of a political candidate. At least the church should supply the members with lists to help them see the evil of this one and the virtue of that one.

But the church cannot and should not attempt to take the place of educated and thoughtful citizens. If voters are too lazy to defend their liberties, the church cannot do it for them. If citizens cannot be bothered with constructing a civilized society, it is not the business of the church to impose one on them. It is the business of the church to preach the Word of God; it is the business of citizens, yes, also of Christian citizens, in a democratic society to construct a civilized society.

The church aids by pointing out, as we did in an earlier chapter, the duty of citizens according to the Word of God. A Christian citizen should be able to determine how that Word applies to each political decision without a road map from his or her pastor.

Let us again call a basic principle to mind: The state does not run on the living water of the Word and sacraments; it runs on the basis of natural law and reason. Those who attempt to influence legislation therefore must do it on the basis of the natural law and reason.

The church, however, operates only with the gospel. Therefore the church as church has no direct role to play in the political arena. That is the business of individual Christians carrying out their role as Christian citizens.

We will rightly assume that when the church is busy with politics, she is not busy with her own work of preaching the gospel. The church should assume that her members can figure out for themselves which candidates best serve the outward good of society and which do not. She should assume that if members are not willing to do their citizenship homework, then they must suffer the consequences of their irresponsibility. In any case, the church cannot and should not do that homework for them. That is not her mission.

The mission of the church is a full-time mission. From the Word of God and even from history, it is very clear what happens when the church treats that mission as a part-time task. Go back and read again the chapters on the history of church-and-state relations. Whenever the two were mixed together in an unscriptural way, there was always a noble motive. And there was also always disaster.

Political activity harms the true mission of the church

Indeed, the church harms her mission when she is diverted from it. For example, in her preaching and teaching, the church condemns most abortions and teaches the doctrine of creation as taught in the Bible.

Now what if the local parish or the church body or church organization formally set out to publicly campaign as a church against abortion and evolution? A woman in the neighborhood hears of the campaign against abortion by the local parish. She had an abortion and is racked with guilt about it, and she should be. Will she or her family ever come to that congregation to hear the gospel? Probably not. The only thing she knows about that congregation is that it opposes abortion; she assumes they oppose her and will reject her.

What if the church gets into a public feud with the local school board over the teaching of evolution? There is no question in our minds that the teaching of evolution has fostered much mischief in our society. That false notion also corrupts what people think about God, about human nature, and about the purpose of life and death. But what happens if the church takes its opposition to evolution on the road, so to speak?

People who never heard the gospel from that church only know one thing about it: It opposes evolution. That one point sticks in their minds whenever they hear of that particular church. Will they come to hear the gospel from a church that seems devoted only to a crusade against evolution? Do we really want that to be what people think of when they hear the name of our church? We teach the doctrine of creation and oppose evolution because the Holy Spirit has convinced us in the gospel that God's Word is true and saving. But the outsider who only hears of us in a political context does not know that. And too many of them never will know it because the church is too busy with politics to be looking for them. Or they will never learn it because they want nothing to do with a church that seems devoted to bashing evolution.

What we believe and teach about evolution or abortion or any other matter is the result of faith worked by the Word. For anyone really to understand our position on all those matters, he or she must first learn of the Savior.

Out of love to him who first loved us, we hold these beliefs on the basis of his Word. The church setting forth only the results of faith in a political arena gets it backwards. First must come the gospel that creates faith; then comes love for Christ who redeemed us; then comes the desire to hold to all his Word. If the church is busy in the political arena, she is busy only with parts of that third element in the chain.

The church must never give the world the impression that the third element is all important. George Unbeliever will never understand the importance of that third element apart from the first two. In fact, George Unbeliever may well say to himself: What point is there in going to church? I already know what it stands for! In point of fact, the political activity of the church got in the way of George ever hearing the gospel.

Individual Christians take their Christianity with them into the political arena; they do not have one set of truths as Christians and a contradictory set as citizens, though the way they make their case is different in the political field than in church.

The church as an institution should not enter the political arena, however. Individual Christians are citizens of the world; the church as Christ's first kingdom is not a citizen of the world, even though she works and serves and suffers in it. The political activity of the individual Christian is not the activity of the church, but of a citizen who is also a Christian.

Called workers of the church and politics

We want to make a clear distinction between church and state. We recognize from the Word of God that the two kingdoms of church and state have very different goals and tools. Therefore we do not want the government to do what God has given the church to do. And we do not want the church to be actively involved in politics.

The desire to keep church and state distinct has implications for the called workers of the church. If the pastor or other called worker runs for public office, what conclusions may people draw from that action? If the pastor signs a petition, even a petition for a good cause, what conclusion might his members and outsiders come to when they see his signature? If the pastor gives an interview on a current political issue that will be published in the newspaper or broadcast on television, what will people think about his church as a result of the interview?

A thoughtful consideration of these questions should produce in called workers of the church the greatest degree of caution about any kind of public political involvement. The pastors and other called workers of our church do not want to do anything that would detract or distract from their work as servants of the gospel.

The pastor signs a petition for the new sewer and water plant. Those who see his signature assume that this is the way the church wants things to go. They may even assume that this is what *God* wants; for after all, that's what the pastor is there for—to tell us what God wants.

Some pastors and teachers become known as political activists for a certain political party. Their churches are opposed to pornography and abortion and the general moral decline in the nation. They want national leaders who can be counted on to stand up for what's right and true and, yes, Christian.

But their association with the political party of their choice means that they also become associated with views of that party that have nothing to do with morality, with right and wrong. By their public alliance with a political movement, do they give people the impression that God wants social security and highway programs and defense spending done in that political party's way? Regardless of how Christian any party's views may seem, compromise is the essence of success in politics. Do pastors and teachers of the church really want to give the impression that God's Word is negotiable?

God gives the sword to the state to govern outward behavior; he gives the church the gospel to change hearts. Pastors and teachers have the gospel for hearts. Why would they want to busy themselves with the sword of the state? That sword on its best day never converted anyone.

Let pastors and teachers occupy themselves with the preaching and teaching they have been called to do as servants of Christ in the midst of the people of God.

The church has any number of organizations inseparably connected to her, such as schools and societies for helping the retarded, unwed mothers, the aged, the troubled, the addicted. Let organizations of the church established to deal with specific problems in society be busy in caring for the needs of their clients; theirs is not a political mission either, even though political problems make their work more difficult.

It is very tempting perhaps for many involved in such work to want to take a legal shortcut that will make their work easier. Perhaps the pro-life organization of the church should lobby or demonstrate against easy abortion laws. Maybe those who work with the aged should start a campaign for increased governmental aid and protection for senior citizens. The parish school board could lobby for this or that advantage for nonpublic schools.

But all who are representing the church need constantly to remember that we imitate Christ in his humiliation; we bear the message of the gospel to those we serve, expecting aggravation, obstacles, frustrations. As Christ refused the shortcut offered by Satan in Matthew 4:9, so too do the public servants of Christ's church. We must leave it to citizens and to Christians as citizens to attend to matters in the political arena; that's not the business of the church; that's not the work of her called servants.

In sum, the called workers of the church may have political views and certainly may exercise their political right to vote. But their political views should not be translated into public political activity. By virtue of their service to the first kingdom, they willingly give up the exercise of some political rights in the second kingdom. Paul wanted his members to think of Christ crucified when they thought of him (1 Corinthians 2:1,2; 2 Corinthians 10:1-5). Our called workers should have the same goal.

The "Christian Right" and the "Christian Left"

The gospel for the church; the sword for the state. Hearts and souls for the church; outward behavior for the state. Eternal life with this life as a pilgrimage for the church; temporal matters and this life as the sole concern for the state. That should be sufficient to keep the church as church out of the Christian right and the Christian left political movements.

Political organizations on both sides, however, are filled with clergy representing God as being in favor of this or that social program. The Christian Coalition represents the "Christian Right." The National Rainbow Coalition represents the "Christian Left." Both these groups want, in one way or another, to improve society under the careful direction of the spokesmen for the church. They all share in some notion of an earthly kingdom of Christ happily united with the heavenly kingdom.

Where is the proper preaching of law and gospel in the Christian Right or the Christian Left? Who thinks of Christ crucified for the sins of the world when they think of the Christian Coalition or the Rainbow Coalition? Though the causes championed by these groups may often be noble and worthy, they are not the chief business of the church. Many of the causes are no business of the church at all.

The proper understanding of the different work God has given to the church and the state is often missing altogether. Likewise, the understanding that there really is no such thing as a Christian society or Christian nation is missing. There are Christians in society and in nations. They live by faith, not by sight; that is, they trust that Christ rules over history and over all the earth. But they do not expect to see the triumph of his rule in this life. They wait, and they imitate Christ's humility. Exaltation comes in the next life, not in this one.

These political groupings of churches and clergy can end up encouraging civil disobedience to the state. They become so frustrated at their inability to reform society according to their version of God's will that they see demonstrations, possibly even riot and mayhem, as legitimate tools in their arsenal from God. What a contradiction that is to all that Christ tells us to do as a church!

In sum: the narrow Lutheran middle road

What should the church do about legalized abortion, rampant gambling, pornography, and the breakdown of family values in schools and on television?

- The church should preach the law and the gospel. That's the work Christ gave her.

- The church should leave it to Christians to translate the law and the gospel into their own political activity.

- The church should urge her members to serve the state.

- The church should call her members to increased devotion to the Word and sacraments in a perishing world.

- The church should remind her members that their true citizenship is in heaven, their temporary visa is in this world.

The whole of the Christian life is a struggle to keep away from false extremes. We are in the world but not of it. We live for heaven while we live on earth. We pray for the state and serve it while knowing all along that the state is temporary and perishing with the world.

As citizens of the earthly kingdom, we do not hide our Christian convictions, even though we know they will be despised by most and cherished by few. When as Christians we debate in the political arena, we do not expect to do so on the basis of the Word of God. We must argue on the basis of reason and natural law when these are in harmony with the Word of God. That debate in the political arena is the business of the Christian as citizen, however; it is not the business of the church.

When the church rebukes sin in society, she does so as part of her prophetic mission in the interest of bringing people to repentance. The church rebukes sin so she can preach the gospel of forgiveness, not promote part of a political action agenda.

Christ is King in both kingdoms. We serve him by trusting him and his Word, especially when it seems all our labors are in vain. We serve him by doing our duty, lest we bring disgrace to his Word and so drive away those who still are perishing for lack of it. Yes, we serve him by making sure the church concerns herself only with the work God gave her, the work of preaching and teaching his Word in all its truth and purity in all the world and administering the sacraments according to his institution.

Endnotes

[1]Large Catechism, Part IV:20, *The Book of Concord: The Confessions of the Evangelical Lutheran Church*, translated and edited by Theodore G. Tappert (Philadelphia: Fortress Press, 1959), p. 439.

[2]Formula of Concord, Epitome, Article XII:14, Tappert, p. 499.

[3]Apology of the Augsburg Confession, Article XVI:7, Tappert, p. 223.

[4]Augsburg Confession, Article XXVIII:10-13, Tappert, pp. 82,83.

[5]Martin Luther, *Luther's Works*, edited by Jaroslav Pelikan and Helmut T. Lehmann, American Edition (St. Louis: Concordia Publishing House; Philadelphia: Fortress Press, 1955–1986), Vol. 46, pp. 155-205.

[6]*Luther's Works*, Vol. 46, pp. 3-85.

[7]Large Catechism, Preface:6, Tappert, p. 359.

For Further Reading

Augsburg Confession, Articles 16 and 28; Apology of the Augsburg Confession, Article 16; Formula of Concord, Epitome, Article XII:12-16. *The Book of Concord: The Confessions of the Evangelical Lutheran Church*. Translated and edited by Theodore G. Tappert. Philadelphia: Fortress Press, 1959.

Brug, John. "The Lutheran Doctrine of the Two Kingdoms." *Our Great Heritage*. Edited by Lyle Lange. Vol. 2. Milwaukee: Northwestern Publishing House, 1991.

Luther, Martin. "Temporal Authority: To What Extent it Should be Obeyed, 1523." *Luther's Works*. Edited by Jaroslav Pelikan and Helmut T. Lehmann. American Edition. Vol. 45. Philadelphia: Fortress Press, 1962.

Scripture Index

Genesis
1,2,—85
2:20—14
2:24—14
3—14,79,80
3:15—14,15,19,35
3:16-19—36
4—14,15
4:10-12—36
4:10-16—15
4:23,24—15
6,7—36,37
6:11-13—15
9:6—15
19—37
41–50—16

Exodus
1—64,67
2:11-15—16

Deuteronomy
5—18
13—19
16:18-20—19
17:8-13—18,19
17:13—20
19:1-13—19
19:21—22
20:1-9—19
21:1-9—19
21:18-21—19
23:19,20—19
24:1-5—19
25:5-10—19

Judges
2–16—37

1 Samuel
15—25
15:1-9,20-23—35

15:23—28
16:1-13—25
22:6-19—26
24—26
26—26

2 Kings
17—28
17:7-23—37
25—28

2 Chronicles
36:15-19—37
36:15-23—28

Psalms
2—47,48
2:8,9—47
17—27
17:13—27
35—27
69—27
109—27
119:105—84

Isaiah
24–27—48
45—48
53—35
55:10,11—54
60–66—48

Jeremiah
25:8-14—37
29:7—30,32

Ezekiel
33—193

Daniel
2—33,48
3—31
3:28,29—32
4:37—32
4—33
5—33
6—31
6:26,27—32

Matthew
2:13-15—56
4:4—165
4:8-10—56
4:9—200
5—18,20,101
5:14,16—70
5:16—27
5:33-37—103
5:38-48—99
6:33—165
7:15—159
10—67
10:17-25—148
10:32,33—66
11:28—53
13:24-30—148
14:22—57
16:18—111
16:21-23—57
16:26—165
17:24-27—62
19:8—20
22:15-21—62
22:21—62
23:37—146
24:6,7—95

25:41,46—36
26:52-54—57
26:63,64—103
26:64—57
26:69-75—103
28:18—8,49
28:18-20—40,54,70,107

Luke
3:14—93
7:9—94
16:19-31—36

John
1:29—36,146
3:16—36,146
6:14,15—57
6:15—57
6:35-40—54
6:68,69—53
10:17,18—57
11:25,26—53
17:15-18—69
18:36—58

Acts
5—64,65
5:29—65
5:42—65
9:16—50
10—94
16:22-40—100
21:27–26:32—100
23:1-5—60

Romans
1—30,82
1:18-23—29

1:18-32—30
2:14,15—29
6:4—53
8:18-39—37
8:31-39—51
10:14-20—54
13—40,43,54,61,62,64
13:1—45,100
13:1-7—39,41,137
13:4—40,41,54,94
13:5—42,62
16:17,18—159

1 Corinthians
2:1,2—201
6:1-8—98
10:16—53
12:3—54
13:12—58

2 Corinthians
5:18-21—36
5:19-21—146
10:1-5—201
10:5—9

Galatians
5:14-26—18
6:10—87

Ephesians
1:18-22—50
1:22,23—8
2:1-5—80
2:8,9—146
5—18
5:22–6:4—40

Philippians
    2:5—55
    2:5-8—55
    2:6-11—49
    2:9-11—56

Colossians
    1:15-18—50
    2:16,17—18

2 Thessalonians
    2:1-12—124

1 Timothy
    2:1,2—62
    2:2—72
    2:3,4—63,72
    6:6-10—165

2 Timothy
    3:16—35

Titus
    3:1—43

1 Peter
    2—64
    2:13,14—43
    2:15-21—71
    2:23—60

1 John
    2:1,2—146

Jude
    3—159

Revelation
    20:11-15—36

Subject Index

abortion 67,78,79,85,86,89,90,
    196,197,200,202
American Revolution 153,154
Athanasius 115
Augsburg Confession 133,134,
    142,154

Babylonian captivity 28-34,52
Bonaparte, Napoleon 155-157

called workers and politics
    198-201
Calvin, John 143-150
Calvinism 143-150
capitalism 164,165
Catholics 132,133,135,136,
    139-141,149,150
ceremonial law 18
chaplains, military 187-189
Charlemagne 122,123
Charles V 132,140,141

Christian Coalition 201
church
    prophetic role of 191-196
    and state aid 185-187
civil disobedience 202
Christian Left 201,202
Christian Right 176-179,201,
    202
civil law 18-23,33,34
communism 162-166
conscientious objector 96,97
consistory 138,139
Constantine 112-118
Constitution, United States
    153,171-176
Council of Nicea 114,115
courts 98-104
Crusades, the 126-131

Daniel 31-34
David 25-28

Edict of Milan 112-114
education 137,138,156-159, 164,173-185
England 149,156,157
Establishment Clause 172-176, 179-185

fall (into sin) 14
First Amendment 171-173, 180,187
Formula of Concord 100,142, 150
Fourteenth Amendment 171, 172
France 149,154,155
Free Exercise Clause 176,179
French Revolution 154,155

gambling 78,202
Germany 132-142,149,150

Hegel, Georg Wilhelm Friedrich, 161,162,164

idolatry 19,31-34
Islam 119,120
Israel 13-23

lawsuits 98,99
Locke, John 153
Luther, Martin 60,61,131-140, 143-146,148

Marx, Karl, 162-164
Marxism 162-166
Montesquieu 153

moral law 18,20-23,30,33,34, 76
Muhlenberg, Henry Melchior 154
murder 15,16,30,94
Muslims 119-121

National Rainbow Coalition 201
natural law 29-32,34,76,81,82, 84,88,195,203
Nicene Creed 115
Ninety-five Theses 131,132

oaths 102-104

Peace of Augsburg 141,142
Peasant's War, the 136,137
persecution 108-120,133,136, 141,154
political activity harms mission of church 196-201
politics 75-91,134,135,162, 193-201
popes 123-128
Prussian Union 159-161
purgatory 127,128,130,131, 140

reason 29-32,34,76-85,88-91, 145,146,153,154,165,195, 203
rebellion 25-28,31-34,42,43, 67, 96
Reformation, the 128,130-133, 138,140,143,152

Religious Left 201,202
Religious Right 176-179,201,
    202
Roman Empire 109,112,116
Rome 120-123
Rousseau, Jean-Jacques 152

schools
    public 77,78,90,157,172-
        180,184
    religious 107,137,156,
        170,171,179-185
    state aid to 179-185
school board 77,78,90,196
Smith, Adam 153

social contract 152-154
soldiers 93-97,110,188
state church 160,172

taxes 41,61,62,119,120,158-
    160,172,179-181,185-187
theology of glory 148
theology of the cross 148
Thirty Years' War 139,149

Voltaire 153
voting 75-79,85-88,194-196

war 34-38,48,93-97
work-righteousness 113